Henry‿ Si

D0863653

Henryk Sienkiewicz

A BIOGRAPHY

Mieczyslaw Giergielewicz

HIPPOCRENE BOOKS
New York

Hippocrene paperback edition, 1991

ISBN 0-87052-118-7

For information, address:
HIPPOCRENE BOOKS, INC.
171 Madison Avenue
New York, NY 10016

Printed in the United States of America

Henryk Sienkiewicz

Historical Background

To assess properly Sienkiewicz's literary standing, some notion of the historical framework may be helpful. The most important event which weighed heavily on the Polish mind and culture in the nineteenth century was the downfall of the Polish-Lithuanian Commonwealth. The causes of this national disaster were widely discussed. Its external reason was the sudden growth of the two military powers: the Prussian Kingdom and the Russian Empire. The danger became acute due to the flaws of the Polish political and social system, which could not withstand the brute efficiency of the neighboring absolute monarchies. At the end of the eighteenth century the alarmed Polish community, inspired by the spirit of the Enlightenment, got rid of the former political prejudices, reorganized education, and in 1791 adopted a new Constitution, but this revival came too late. The lands of Poland were divided among Russia, Prussia, and also Austria, which joined the deal for the sake of political balance.

The Poles were keenly aware of their national distinctiveness and heritage. They could not get reconciled with the loss of political independence. Besides increased efforts in the economic and cultural sphere, they endeavored to regain freedom by armed struggle. On the eve of the final partition of Poland Kosciuszko started an unsuccessful insurrection. Later the Poles associated themselves with Napoleon, hoping for his help, and took part in many of his campaigns. Although the French Emperor suffered a defeat, the role of the Polish troops was not ignored, and at the Congress of Vienna a curtailed Polish Kingdom was established under the rule of the Russian Tsar, while Austria and Prussia retained the major part of their Polish possessions acquired as a result of the partitions.

The Constitution of the newly created Kingdom, more liberal than the regime within Russia, was not respected. The Poles resumed their active resistance, hoping for some international intervention. The rising of 1830–31 stirred European opinion, but did not receive any military assistance, and was suppressed by the Russians. In 1846 another rising broke out in the Austrian partition; but the Austrian administration stirred up a rebellion of the peasants against the gentry, and the subsequent slaughter paralyzed the patriots. The riots in 1848 against the Prussians were also stifled.

Notwithstanding these calamities, Polish literature reached unprecedented excellence. The leading poets—Adam Mickiewicz, Juliusz Slowacki, Cyprian Norwid, Zygmunt Krasinski—joined the political emigration and published their works abroad, mainly in France. They were considered not only artists but also political leaders and spiritual guides. Their poetry, based upon Romantic ideals, proclaimed heroism, self-sacrifice, and devotion to universal freedom. Many other successful writers lived in Poland; their writings were more moderate and reflected more faithfully the needs of the population. Among them Jozef Ignacy Kraszewski, a prolific novelist, enjoyed general acclaim.

Another Polish rising in 1863 met with some lip-service support from France, but the sympathy for Poles was limited to vain protests, and Russia crushed the insurgents mercilessly. The consequences of this defeat were disastrous. The Russians subjected the whole community to cruel revenge and took steps to erase the Polish language and culture. A similar policy was adopted by the Prussian administration which spared no effort to Germanize the Poles and bought their land for German colonists. On the other hand, the Austrians defeated by Prussia introduced in their state a liberal tactic admitting the Poles to the administration and granting them cultural autonomy. Owing to these changes, speedy progress was reached in education, sciences and learning, and Cracow and Lwow became the important centers of Polish cultural life.

In spite of growing Russian repressions, the former Polish Kingdom, with Warsaw as its capital, maintained its leading role. However, political programs were subjected to radical reversals. The publicists condemned reckless military adventures which ended inevitably in vain bloodshed and the waste of national resources. Instead, they recommended the Positivist program. Its elements were based on the works of some Western thinkers, e.g., Comte and Spencer, but were adapted to the situation of the Polish community. It advocated economic, social, and industrial development, as well as increased emphasis on education. The new *credo* penetrated all sections of Poland, with some local modifications.

Romantic dreams were now ridiculed and derided. Writers were expected to keep pace with existing conditions and to co-operate with the protagonists of Positivist objectives. Their duty was to propagate sober practicality, to wage a campaign against social injustice, to weed out the harmful traditions hampering progress, and to foster creative initiatives. The ground for fiction was well prepared by the newspapermen and publicists who attacked their Romantic predecessors, attributing to them all calamities suffered by the nation.

Drama and poetry fell into disrepute, and the novel became the most successful literary genre. Eliza Orzeszkowa valiantly fought for the rights of women and the elimination of social barriers harmful to mutual cooperation. Boleslaw Prus (pseudonym of Alexander Glowacki) made his debut as *feuilletonist* and author of short stories; in his more mature years he wrote several novels portraying the contemporary Polish community; his only historical novel raised the perennial problem of the conflict between power and passion. Together with Sienkiewicz, Prus enjoyed popular acclaim.

Life did not quite meet the hopes nurtured by the Positivist generation. Social progress was slower than had been anticipated; the growth of capitalism contributed to the clashes for which no remedy was in store. Attempts at peaceful coexistence with the hostile occupants produced disappointment. The aging novelists lost their former emotional appeal, and some of them dissociated themselves from certain aspects of the Positivist doctrine. Symbolism, which became the fashion of the day, restored the fascination of the Romantic masters and reinstated poetry and drama to their proper place. The riots of 1905 during the Russo-Japanese war were indicative of the new spirit of the population; their failure did not hinder the secret preparations for a decisive military contest. World War I revived the Polish cause in an international political perspective.

Preface

By the end of the nineteenth century Sienkiewicz had attained universal acclaim. His works were avidly read not only in his native land but also in Western Europe, in Russia, and in America. Scores of reviewers discussed his books immediately after their publication, comparing them with recognized masterpieces. A subsequent partial eclipse did not erase his phenomenal success, even though it reduced the universal response to his work.

Strangely enough, this writer, whose vogue was so widespread, aroused many violent and bitter controversies. They started in the early period of his literary career, continued during his lifetime, and did not subside after his passing. Strife was most obstinate among the author's own countrymen, yet disagreements exploded in several other countries where his popularity reached its peak—France, Italy, and even the United States. The differences of opinion referred to Sienkiewicz's views as well as to some aspects of his technique. This stirring quality of his works could be considered as his additional contribution to literary life.

For many years research on Sienkiewicz was hampered by lack of an authoritative edition of his writings. The gap was filled in post-war Poland by the publication of *Dziela* (Works) in sixty volumes. This tremendous task was completed by Julian Krzyzanowski. The last four volumes brought invaluable marginal data: a calendar of the novelist's life and writings (Vol. LVII, reprinted separately in 1956 and 1957), a bibliography of the novelist's publications and translations into other languages (Vols. LVIII and LIX), and a register of writings on Sienkiewicz (Vol. LX, including over 3800 items).

This impressive achievement coincided with a growing interest in the novelist among the Poles. Once more he became the most popular writer and was eagerly sought by average readers. His revival met at first with some reluctance. There was a brief period after World War II when the exponents of "Socialist Realism" subjected his writings to castigation. However, nothing could stifle the author's spontaneous appeal, and the state indicated its approval. Recently, much valuable research has been done, contributing to a fuller and deeper understanding of the novelist's art.

The present volume is not a biography. Biographical information, provided on a limited scale, was reduced mainly to such facts which could be helpful in clarifying or enriching some aspects of the writer's books. Attention was focused on literary works. No attempt was made to make their review exhaustive; works of minor importance were bypassed (e.g., some of the earlier stories and the plays). In order to do justice to the novelist, he was often shown against a comparative background.

The question, how? appeared more frequently than the questions, who? or what? As a result, various technical features of Sienkiewicz's narrative craft had to be examined. The limited space made it imperative to limit remarks to essentials, accordingly. Various connections with the author's social and national background were also considered, as important ingredients of the texture of his literary fiction.

Much had to be said on Sienkiewicz's association with America —for many reasons. The years of his stay on American soil exerted a profound and prolonged influence on his views and on his creative writing. His enthusiastic reception by American readers was instrumental in creating the writer's international fame and influence. In 1900, President Gilman of Johns Hopkins did not hesitate to announce that the Polish novelist's name was a household word in thousands of American homes. Over 250 editions of Sienkiewicz's books were absorbed by the American people; millions of copies have circulated among the adults and the youth. Such a response can be slighted or exalted, viewed with regret or appreciation; but it should not be ignored.

In the present book I feel indebted to many writers and scholars who made it possible. Especially, the debt to Julian Krzyzanowski cannot be overestimated. I am grateful to the personnel of the Library of the University of Pennsylvania and the New York Public Library for their services. I thank the Polish Library in

Preface

London and its indefatigable Chief Librarian, Mrs. Maria Danile-wicz, for special courtesies; to Professors Ludwik Krzyzanowski and Adam Gillon for their patient editorial guidance; and to Mr. Walter Kondy for his devoted assistance in editing the book. I express my gratitude to Little, Brown & Co., Publishers, for permission to quote fragments of their editions of Sienkiewicz's works; and to Professor Charles Morley and the Columbia University Press for a similar kindness.

November 1965.

MIECZYSLAW GIERGIELEWICZ

University of Pennsylvania

Contents

Chronology

1846   Henryk Sienkiewicz born May 5, uncle's home in Wola Okrzejska, Podlasie, Poland; son of Jozef and Stefania Cieciszowska Sienkiewicz.

1858   Began high school education in Warsaw.

1865–   Worked as tutor; prepared for and passed final examina-
1866   tion; entered faculty of law, University of Warsaw; changed to medicine.

1867   Transferred to Department of History and Literature.

1869   Published review of a play by Sardou and essay on Mikolaj Sep Szarzynski, Polish sixteenth-century poet.

1871   Left university without taking finals.

1872   Novel *In Vain* serialized in biweekly *Wieniec* (Garland); began work as journalist.

1873   Contributed *feuilletons* to *Gazeta Polska;* departed in July for Vienna to report on local exhibition.

1874   Took first longer trip abroad to Ostend and Paris.

1875   Wrote short novel *Hania.*

1876   Left for United States, February 19, as correspondent to describe country for *Gazeta Polska* and prepare for colony in California planned by Modjeska, her husband, and friends; accompanied actress on triumphal tour of American stage; published article in California newspaper; wrote *Charcoal Sketches,* other short stories, and *American Letters.*

1878   Returned in April to Western Europe for one year; stayed mainly in Paris.

1879   Wrote *Orso* and *Yanko the Musician;* delivered lectures on his American impressions; in Italy wrote *From the Memoirs of a Poznan Tutor* and *After Bread.*

1880   First collective edition of his writings printed.

1881   Married Maria Szetkiewicz.

1882   Edited Warsaw daily, *Slowo,* in which he published

Recollections of Mariposa, Bartek the Conqueror; son Henryk born in July.

1883 Published American short story, *Sachem;* instalments of *With Fire and Sword* appear in *Slowo* (Warsaw), *Czas* (Cracow); daughter Jadwiga born in December.

1884 Published *With Fire and Sword* as book, with second edition in July; traveled because of wife's health; serialized *The Deluge* simultaneously in Warsaw, Cracow, and Poznan.

1885 Continued work on *The Deluge;* wife died October 19.

1886 Completed *The Deluge;* journeyed to Rumania, Bulgaria, Turkey, and Greece.

1887 Commenced work on *Pan Michael* and printed instalments in same dailies as *The Deluge;* resigned as editor of *Slowo.*

1888 Completed *Pan Michael* in May; excursion to Spain; wrote *The Third One.*

1889 Wrote essay *On the Historical Novel;* began *Without Dogma.*

1890 Finished *Without Dogma;* took part in transfer of Mickiewicz's ashes; wrote *Lux in Tenebris Lucet* and *The Verdict of Zeus;* departed for Africa; Curtin published English translation of *With Fire and Sword.*

1891 Traveled in Egypt; left Zanzibar for safari in Central Africa; ill with malaria; returned to Europe and wrote *Letters from Africa.*

1892 Wrote *Let Us Follow Him;* began *The Polaniecki Family.*

1893 Married Maria Romanowska; separated shortly thereafter, and marriage later annulled.

1894 Completed *The Polaniecki Family.*

1895 Began *Quo Vadis?* in Nice; commenced *The Teutonic Knights* which took four years.

1898 Requested postponement of the 25th anniversary jubilee of his literary career and concentrated on Mickiewicz Centennial; published address for unveiling of poet's monument in Warsaw.

1900 Sienkiewicz's jubilee solemnized in Poland and abroad; received Oblegorek estate as national gift; wrote speech on Slowacki.

Chronology

1901   First rumors of novelist's candidacy for Nobel Prize; signed contract for *On the Field of Glory*.

1903   Met for the last time Jeremiah Curtin, American translator, at Oblegorek; started *On the Field of Glory*.

1904   Wed Maria Babska, May 5.

1905   Awarded Nobel Prize.

1906   Wrote protests against Prussian resolution to dispossess Polish landowners.

1908   Published *The Verdict of Osiris*.

1909   Completed *Whirlpools;* wrote obituary of H. Modjeska; took active part in Slowacki Centennial.

1911   Resumed idea, conceived 1895, of novel on Polish legions in Napoleonic campaigns; writing interrupted by war.

1914   Left Oblegorek for Cracow, then Vienna, and finally settled in neutral Switzerland; appointed, October 3, full member by Academy of Arts and Sciences in Petersburg.

1915   Joined Central Swiss Committee for Victims of War in Poland, of which he became chairman; started widespread relief work by publishing appeals to Poles and other nations; cooperated with Paderewski; corresponded with Romain Rolland.

1916   Secured participation of Poles in Shakespeare Memorial Book; died of arteriosclerosis, November 15, in Vevey.

1924   October, ashes of novelist brought to Poland and interred in crypt of St. John's Cathedral, Warsaw.

1929   Beginning of publication of Sienkiewicz's collective works, edited by Ignacy Chrzanowski (46 vols. were published).

1948– New sixty-volume edition, edited by Julian Krzyzanowski,
1955   published.

CHAPTER 1

Life and Laurels

I *Family and Education*

WHEN Henryk Sienkiewicz became a celebrity, his foreign visitors sometimes described him as a perfect representative of the Polish aristocracy, inferior to none in Europe. In 1925, an American biographer wrote that the novelist belonged to a "Patrician" family, whatever this appellation was meant to signify.[1] However, the writer's origin was not so dignified. His paternal ancestors were Lithuanian Tatars; the Sienkiewicz clan lived in the eastern provinces of the Polish-Lithuanian state. Chiefly soldiers, one of them, Michal, was baptized in 1740 and elevated to the rank of a noble in 1775 by the Polish Sejm (Diet).[2] Henryk Sienkiewicz was his great-grandson. Henryk's grandfather served in the Napoleonic Army. Eventually, he became Senior State Forester, and he also owned a small estate. He had three sons, one of whom, named Jozef was the father of the future writer. Jozef was called the "heir of Grotki" and earned his living as leaseholder of small estates. He, too, had military experience as he took part in the Insurrection of 1831.

Jozef Sienkiewicz was not a wealthy man; but his financial situation and social standing improved owing to his marriage in 1843 with Stefania Cieciszowska, whose connections with nobility were more pronounced.[3] Among her relatives were a few outstanding intellectuals, such as Jadwiga Luszczewska (pseudonym, "Deotyma"), a poet admired for her gift of versified improvisations, and Joachim Lelewel, a renowned historian and politician.

The couple's first son, Kazimierz (1844–71), died at Orleans during the Franco-Prussian War. The future writer was born on May 7, 1846, in Wola Okrzejska near Siedlce in Russian-occupied

Poland. At baptism, he received the names Henryk Adam Aleksander Pius, but he used only the first one. Henryk had one brother and four sisters. In 1855, his parents purchased an estate in the Mazovian Province. When the children reached school age, the parents sold the estate and bought an apartment house in Praga, a Warsaw suburb. This new investment did not produce the expected income. Moreover, whatever extra money could be accumulated had to be put aside for the dowry of their four daughters.

Henryk's early childhood was spent mainly in the country where he frequently heard stories of family military traditions. During the time he lived with his relatives in Wola Okrzejska, he perused various ancient books and pamphlets he found there; in this way he became acquainted with Polish literature and history. Then too, like many other children, he admired *Robinson Crusoe* and the *Swiss Family Robinson* and even dreamed of settling on an uninhabited island. A biography of Napoleon also made a strong impression on the boy. He began to write prose and verse, but as yet he did not entertain the idea of becoming a writer.[4]

While attending secondary school in Warsaw, he was attracted more by Sir Walter Scott and Alexander Dumas than by his textbooks. He was an average pupil, but he excelled in Polish language and history. For some reason, probably financial, he left school without obtaining a certificate of graduation and became a tutor on an estate. At that time, he allegedly wrote his youthful novel *Ofiara* (The Sacrifice). Finally, in 1866, he submitted to the required final examinations, which he passed. Following his mother's desire, he entered Warsaw University to study law but soon changed to medicine. In February 1867, he was permitted to transfer to history and literature. Like many of his student friends, he lived in poverty; his income was mostly derived from tutoring.[5]

Warsaw University, called *Szkola Glowna* (Main School), had been established in 1862 during a brief period of a more liberal trend of the tsarist administration. Its autonomous existence was short-lived, for in 1869 the Russians closed it. It reappeared as the Imperial University, with Russian as the required language. Despite its brief existence as a Polish institution of higher learning, Warsaw University made a valuable contribution to learning and science, and its students distinguished themselves in various fields. Although the faculty adhered to the philosophical traditions of the earlier period, the young students were eager to establish close contact with contemporary European thought. Among their idols were Auguste Comte, John Stuart Mill, Charles Darwin, Herbert Spencer, Henry Burke, and the materialists Karl Vogt, Jacob Moleschott, and Ludwig Büchner.

II *Ideologies*

Sienkiewicz's university studies coincided with one of the saddest periods in Polish history. After the disastrous Insurrection of 1863, the tsarist regime intensified its campaign to Russianize the Polish people. It subjected the Poles to relentless pressure in both the cultural and economic spheres. The frustrated intellectuals who came to the conclusion that the past methods of resistance were responsible for the national calamity, proclaimed that planned education and peaceful, systematic, and arduous work should replace armed rebellion and clandestine conspiracies. As the main goals of the community, they recommended technical progress, social development, and wealth. Since they considered the underprivileged classes of burghers and peasants as the mainstay of national survival, they pointed out the urgent necessity to "work at the foundations." Publicists condemned the reckless outbursts of national energy and counseled "organic work," which was slower but continuous and embraced all aspects of national life.

This doctrine of Positivism came from the West, but its Polish version depended primarily on local conditions. Some circumstances favored the program. First of all, the belated growth of industry, concurrent with developments in the West, produced changes in the social structure and increased the power of finance. The abolition of customs-duties between Poland and Russia intensified mutual commerce. The emancipation of the peasants

[23]

reduced the role of the gentry, paved the way for an influx of people to the cities, and made imperative the advancement of general education.

The proponents of the new program assigned a different role to literature. The former lofty flights were to be abandoned in favor of serving the practical, everyday needs of the community. Writers were expected to practice realism and to cooperate with the efforts begun in other fields; to fight against outdated traditions, prejudices, and superstitions; to erase unearned privileges; to defend the injured, destitute, and humiliated; and to promote Positivist designs. Only didactic works met with approval. Idleness and dreams were ridiculed and censured. Instead of chivalrous enthusiasts, heroic knights of freedom, and inspired artists, the writers exalted productive engineers and scientists, successful businessmen, skillful physicians, and brave educators.

Although Sienkiewicz was not a frequent guest at student gatherings, he could not remain indifferent to the ideas stirring his generation. Even though he treated them more coolly than the spokesmen of the Positivist movement and abstained from writing militant articles supporting their program, these ideas became a part of his intellectual equipment.

While yet a student, his early novel *Na marne* (In Vain), which at first appeared in the fortnightly *Wieniec* (Garland) in 1872, was a reflection of the author's immediate surroundings. Its setting was Kiev, but the students introduced by Sienkiewicz were not unlike his Warsaw colleagues.[6] Despite some defects, it earned the approbation of the veteran writer Jozef Ignacy Kraszewski, who called it a true reflection of life and found it worthy of being printed. Another work, entitled *Humoreski z teki Worszylly* (Humoresques from Worszyllo's Portfolio, 1872), was more outspoken and was written in a satirical vein.

Sienkiewicz's studies ended in June 1871, but he refrained from taking all final examinations. He turned to journalism and began contributing reviews of current events and occasional essays to various newspapers and periodicals. After 1873, he submitted to *Gazeta Polska*, under the *nom de plume* "Litwos," his weekly "Kroniki" (Chronicles), a kind of *feuilletons* in which he discussed in an entertaining way the petty episodes of ordinary life and urgent social needs. He was occasionally required to visit various provincial cities as a reporter, and his first trip abroad took him to Vienna, where he wrote a report on the exhibition held there at the time. When his friends Godlewski and Ochorowicz purchased the moderately progressive weekly *Niwa* (Field) in 1874, Sienkiewicz began to edit its literary section. With the help of two other friends, he translated Victor Hugo's novel *Quatre-vingt-treize*. For a time, he lived abroad in Ostend and Paris. In 1875 he returned to Warsaw and worked as a regular "chronicler" for *Gazeta Polska*.

III *Visit to America*

Gradually his circle of acquaintances grew. Several friends recorded in their memoirs various details concerning their contacts with the future novelist. The actress Helena Modjeska was one of these. Sienkiewicz, who sincerely admired her acting, was glad to meet her, as well as her husband Karol Chlapowski, at the country house of Edward Leo, a lawyer and editor of *Gazeta Polska*.[7] Modjeska became one of Sienkiewicz's good friends, and the novelist often attended her Tuesday receptions. The actress drew a vivid portrait of the writer in her memoirs.[8]

According to Modjeska, the idea of a trip to the United States was conceived in her drawing room. At one of her Tuesday parties toward the close of 1875, someone brought news of the forthcoming Centennial Exhibition in Philadelphia. Sienkiewicz began to describe America in glowing colors. A Dr. Karwowski entered the room just as Sienkiewicz's tale reached its climax and said jokingly to the hostess, "You need a change of air, Madame. Why not make a trip to America?" "That's a good idea," her husband answered. One of the guests laughed and exclaimed, "Let us all go. We will kill beasts, build huts, make our own garments of skin, and live as our fathers lived!" All laughed, and the idea was dismissed as an impossibility.[9]

In fact, the project of such an expedition created a great deal of excitement. Rudolf (Ralph), Modjeska's son by a former marriage, dreamed of such a trip, for he wanted to help build the Panama Canal. Chlapowski felt that a long voyage might restore his wife's health. The actress was weary of the jealousy and petty intrigues she had had to endure in Warsaw, and perhaps she secretely dreamed of playing Shakespeare in the original language. There might also have been some kind of romantic association with the writer; if so, it remained a well-guarded secret and was never confirmed.[10]

The political situation also played an important role in their decision. The pressure of the administration grew stronger after the death of Mme Maria Kalergis-Mukhanov, the wife of the Russian administrator of the Warsaw theaters, who was Modjeska's devoted admirer; clashes with the censors became more annoying. Modjeska's friends "used to talk about the new country, the new life, new scenery . . . away from daily vexations to which every Pole was exposed in Russian or Prussian Poland." Sienkiewicz was "the first to advocate emigration. Little by little others followed him, and soon five of them expressed the desire to seek adventures in the jungles of the virgin land."[11]

Modjeska's husband, infected by the enthusiasm of the younger men, developed the idea of a colony in California reminiscent of Brook Farm, which had been established in West Roxbury, Massachusetts, in 1841 in accordance with the Socialist doctrine of Fourier. The volunteers planned the details of the expedition and drew up rules, which they promised to obey. "What wild dreams we dreamt!" exclaimed Modjeska in her *Memories,* "What visions of freedom, peace, and happiness flitted across my brains! I was to give up the stage and live in the midst of nature, perhaps in a tent! I pictured to myself a life of toil under the blue skies of California, among the hills, riding on horseback with a gun over my shoulder. . . . What joy—I thought—to bleach linen at the brook like the maidens of Homer's *Iliad!*"[12]

The news of their prospective departure created a mild sensation in Warsaw. *Gazeta Polska* agreed to pay Sienkiewicz's expenses. According to the formal communiqué issued by the press, the author left to visit the Philadelphia Centennial Exhibition as correspondent. Sienkiewicz's real task was to locate a suitable place for the settlement in California and to report on his American impressions. After an amicable luncheon, Sienkiewicz and his friend Juliusz Sypniewski began their long journey on

February 19, 1876.[13] In London their guide was the writer Ignacy Maciejowski ("Sewer"). On February 24 they began their voyage across the Atlantic Ocean.

From the very beginning of his stay in America, which preceded by a few years the trip of the Norwegian Knut Hamsun, Sienkiewicz set down his impressions in order to prepare the reports in the form of letters. During his first few months, he found everything shocking and abhorrent; but later, as he grew accustomed to his surroundings, his attitude changed:

... now I have to restrain my sympathy as I feel that my emotions are not preconceived or prearranged, but on the contrary, in spite of my former prejudices capture my heart by an assault. I can briefly say that I feel so well here that if I were sure of eternal life I would not like to spend it elsewhere. You promised me some advantageous financial conditions in a new publication. I reply to you that I discovered a rare land in this world where people look at money as something which serves for God knows what."[14]

These remarks were written from California, where Sienkiewicz arrived on March 16, 1876. He spent several days in San Francisco, where he visited the local Polish colony. His new acquaintances were Julian Horain, a journalist who had lived in the United States since 1871, and a number of political émigrés. He lived in their homes and listened avidly to their yarns. A most remarkable figure among them was the seventy-five-year-old Captain Rudolf Korwin Piotrowski, a still-vigorous and cheerful man. He was an ingenious storyteller and excelled in concocting fantastic lies, especially with regard to his amorous adventures; and he did not shun liquor. When his doctor ordered him to drink milk, he dutifully obeyed, but mixed it sparingly with whiskey. Sienkiewicz, who was fond of the old man, drew a sketch of him and promised to immortalize him in his writings.

From San Francisco the novelist moved to Anaheim in Southern California. He chose a suitable location for the farm and prepared for the arrival of the settlers. Sienkiewicz also found time to make occasional excursions to Los Angeles and to the mountains to hunt big game. He became acquainted with the adventurer Max Neblung, the Liedtke family, and several Spanish ladies. At the same time, he did not neglect his writing. As of May 1876, his American letters began appearing in *Gazeta Polska*. He also wrote a five-act play called *By Force* (later changed to *Na jedna karte*, On a Single Card). He regularly received periodicals and books from Poland and attentively followed literary developments there.

During his travels across the North American continent, Sienkiewicz had some adventures that he duly reported to his friends. In a letter to Stefania Leo, he thanked her for the chocolates she had given him in Warsaw and which helped to establish friendly contact with some Indian natives whom he had met in Ketchum:

The last but one portion with some tobacco, I gave to an Indian of the Sioux tribe at the station in Ketchum and for this gift the red-skinned fellow declared, "My brother is a great warrior as his hand is open, his face is pale but his heart is red." Later, a French translator who knew English assured me that the war hatchet between me and my tribe on the one hand, and the Sioux on the other would be buried forever, and so forth. So your chocolates not only provided me with a long-lasting and tasteful refreshment but owing to it I became a great warrior (of which I never dreamed) and concluded an eternal alliance with the noble nation of the Sioux. This alliance is even more precious to me, as at the belt of the warrior with whom I spoke hung several scalps, evidently recently torn off some skulls. The belligerent Sioux were present in Ketchum for negotiations with the railway administration. I liked them very much and all my sympathy was on their side.[15]

Living with nature and the endurance of outdoor hardships improved Sienkiewicz's health and stamina. He expressed self-confidence in a letter to Lubowski:

My attire consisting of a flannel shirt, red pants, and a sombrero cost one dollar. The climate does not require anything else. At night I have a blanket over me and plenty of skins underneath; I sleep at a fire made of—guess what?—laurel twigs. I got rid of my nerves, my catarrh, my toothache. I sleep like a king. A linen roof over my head I consider effeminacy and only necessary during rain. Until now the hardship of this Cossak life only strengthens me; I do not know whether some reaction will follow and whether I shall not collapse under the burden.

But in the meantime I am as healthy as a bull, much stronger than my red brothers, cheerful and happy. Every morning when I wake up, I remind myself where I am and I can't restrain a smile of sincere satisfaction. I get up to face life with a smile.[16]

In the meantime, preparations for the settlement were progressing smoothly. Sienkiewicz advised the purchase of land not far from the city. He rented a temporary house and bought necessary equipment. He was pleased to report to his Warsaw friends that the price of land was low and that it would be easy for the Polish settlers to earn a living. Sypniewski, who returned to Europe in order to give an oral report, spoke enthusiastically about the prospects of the planned colony and thus removed any possible hesitations of the colonists.

At last, in September 1876, Modjeska, her husband, her son, and three companions arrived in California. For some time she stayed in San Francisco, while other members of the party went directly to Anaheim. Sienkiewicz especially welcomed two large trunks containing about one thousand books. He hoped that the colony would become a little Athens.[17] However, the project of establishing a permanent settlement was doomed from the start. Its participants lacked the necessary knowledge of practical agriculture and were unaccustomed to physical exertion. The initial enchantment did not last long, and nostalgia soon gnawed at the hearts of the voluntary exiles. Mutual harmony disappeared, especially when Chlapowski and his wife noticed that their funds were almost exhausted; the establishment grew costlier than they had anticipated. Modjeska began to learn English and was ready in a few months to resume her theatrical career on American soil. In the meantime, the writer worked hard on a drama based on American life. He made many changes but he did not finish it (only some fragments survived).[18]

Since Chlapowski was seemingly jealous of Sienkiewicz, the writer's stay at the colony became awkward and uncomfortable. For several weeks he lived in San Francisco, eagerly awaiting the stage appearances of Modjeska. There, he became an accidental witness to a murder and helped to capture the killer. The victim was a New York banker; his murderer, the consul of Guatemala. Sienkiewicz was subpoenaed and was told to remain in the city until the trial. However, his patience was not exposed to a severe test since the murderer committed suicide the following day.

Gazeta Polska printed Sienkiewicz's *Charcoal Sketches* which provoked a heated discussion. The author planned a whole series of satirical tales written in the same mood. He continued to submit his American letters regularly to the paper. After Modjeska's debut in one of the San Francisco theaters on August 20, 1877, he enthusiastically reported to his Polish readers the actress' fantastic success on the American stage. Exploiting the public's favorable reception, he wrote a political essay for the San Francisco *Daily Evening Post* on Poland, which was warmly praised by Modjeska. It was translated into English and anonymously published on September 8 under the title "Poland and Russia, The Tsar's Government in Poland and on the Danube."[19]

IV *Return to Europe*

In the final weeks of his California period, Sienkiewicz wrote a few essays and short stories based on American life, such as "The Comedy of Errors" and "The Chinese in California." When Modjeska went on a tour of the East, he followed her; he saw her triumphal performances in Boston, Pittsburgh, and New York. In March 1878, he departed for Europe and arrived in London in April. Because of the Russo-Turkish War, he was subject to being drafted into the Tsarist Army; for this reason, he preferred to remain abroad. He lived in Paris for a year where he met many of his countrymen, particularly journalists and artists. *Gazeta Polska* asked him to cover the Paris Exhibition, which he did. Another Warsaw daily, *Nowiny* (News), edited by Erazm Piltz, invited him to send his sketches. Sienkiewicz approved of its progressive moderation and considered joining its editorial staff, since his contacts with *Gazeta Polska* had cooled considerably. The writer was angered by the refusal of the editor of this daily to print one of his sketches which was allegedly antireligious. A reconciliation took place at a later date.[20]

Sienkiewicz continued to draw on his recent American impressions in works of fiction; he wrote the tales "Przez stepy" (translated as "Lillian Morris") and "Orso." He was disappointed that his play *On a Single Card* did not receive an award at a competition in his homeland. However, one of the theaters in Lwow performed it with some success, and soon it appeared in other cities. The writer also turned to short stories dealing with a Polish background, such as "Janko muzykant" and "Jamiol."

In April 1879, the novelist returned to Poland, stopping in Lwow, one of the cultural centers in the Austrian section of Poland. He made a number of friends in literary circles and gave lectures on his American impressions at the city hall.[21] With a similar purpose he visited a few resorts. His negotiations with the editors concerning the collective edition of his works proved successful, and the first volume of *Pisma* appeared in October 1879. While in Lwow, Sienkiewicz printed a few of his short stories in the local newspapers and periodicals.

Rather than return to Warsaw, the writer traveled to Italy, where he spent some time in Venice. Here he met three attractive young ladies: Maria and Jadwiga Szetkiewicz, and Maria Sobotkiewicz. Maria Szetkiewicz would become his wife. The other two became his devoted friends with whom he maintained a correspondence lasting many years. On various occasions, Jadwiga advised the novelist regarding his works, for he relied on her common sense.

After almost four years of absence, Sienkiewicz returned to Warsaw on November 7, 1879. The publication of his collected works enhanced his literary stature, but he still worked as a journalist. He contributed weekly "chronicles" for *Niwa* and wrote "Current News" for *Gazeta Polska*. Warsaw readers were impressed with his new tale "Niewola tatarska" (The Tartar Captivity) in which the writer turned from contemporary problems to the past. This change seemed ominous and aroused some misgivings in the progressive camp.

Meanwhile, Sienkiewicz's courtship of Maria Szetkiewicz was opposed by the girl's parents. There was talk that the writer lacked a secure position and money. Besides, Maria's health caused much anxiety; the doctors advised her to take the cure for tuberculosis in Tyrol. Nonetheless, when the novelist asked for her hand in marriage, his proposal was accepted, and the wedding took place on August 18, 1881. Now Sienkiewicz entered the happiest and most productive period of his career. The influence of his wife was beneficial; she stabilized his life, strengthened his self-confidence, and doubled his working ability. It was not until after this marriage that Sienkiewicz embarked upon his major novels. Then too, his new works revealed a brighter approach, in contrast to his earlier fiction in which a strain of pessimism prevailed.

When in 1882, the liberal conservatives of Warsaw began to publish the new daily *Slowo*, they appointed Sienkiewicz as its editor. In the first year of its publication the daily contained his weekly "chronicles," book reviews, theater criticisms, and short stories. Among the tales were "Bartek zwyciezca" (Bartek the Conqueror), "Wspomnienia z Maripozy" (Recollections of Mariposa), and "Z puszczy bialowieskiej" (From the Bialowieza Forest). As the author's opinion of the peasants under Prussian domination aroused some criticism, he went to Poznan to establish direct contact with the local community and to study conditions. After this visit, he never lost sight of the specific needs of the western provinces.

Sienkiewicz encountered difficulties with some of his former colleagues, who resented his association with the conservatives. However, the author stressed on various occasions that he maintained an independent position. He did not wish to align himself with the views of the bigoted clerical-dominated aristocracy.

... some signs of dissatisfaction regarding the tendency of *Slowo* reached me from Cracow. I have to warn you that even in the future the newspaper will not adopt a color more pleasing to Cracow. Our situation is different and we, local people who are better acquainted with it, must take care not to divide society, not to create hostile camps but rather to unite them for the sake of reasonable progress and love of country.[22]

In July, 1882, Mrs. Sienkiewicz gave birth to a son, named Henryk Jozef, and the financial needs of the family increased. Her husband found a way to raise his income by publishing his writings simultaneously in two newspapers, each in a different city. His major works began to appear in brief instalments. One of the advantages of this scheme was the parallel availability of the same works in the Russian and Austrian occupation. Later, the writer was to make a similar arrangement with a daily in Poznan in the Prussian partition.

V *The Novelist*

The following year, Sienkiewicz focused his energy almost exclusively on his first long historical novel, *With Fire and Sword*. For years he had been preparing himself for this formidable task.

. . . Of my novel, I can only say that I prepared its historical background most thoroughly and I read a great number of contemporary sources, so that I did not take from my imagination a single name. I also attempted to render faithfully the coloring of the era concerned. Things which may look rough are only a reflection of the historical epoch.[23]

Proofreading of the instalments printed in the various papers was imperfect, and many errors marred the finished product. The author was also concerned with the correctness of his Ukrainian quotations and demanded a revision of the text by Bykowski, a novelist born in Podolia, who knew the language. Despite these shortcomings, the novel was considered by the public a tremendous literary achievement.

The revised version, published in book form, became extremely popular. Some readers thought that the characters in the narrative were so authentic that they even prayed for them. Pithy sayings in the text soon became proverbial. Amateur actors drew motifs from it for staging "living pictures." Critics in the progressive camp, although appreciating the novel's artistic aspect, castigated Sienkiewicz's interpretation of historical events and the general idea of the work. On the other hand, its enthusiasts expressed unreserved admiration. Professor Stanislaw Tarnowski, a renowned historian of literature at Cracow University, devoted to the novel a series of lectures. Suddenly, Sienkiewicz found himself in the limelight as a leading writer of his generation.

With the birth of her daughter Jadwiga on December 13, 1883, Maria Sienkiewicz's health grew steadily worse; she suffered from consumption. Her doctor advised her to move to a better climate. The next year the family went to San Remo where some improvement in her health was observed. Two months later, they moved to a French resort and then visited Ostend (in Belgium) and Reichenhall (in Germany). The year 1884 was a busy one for the writer, who went on with the second part of his trilogy *Potop* (The Deluge). When the first instalments came out, the novel was as yet not far advanced, with the result that the prepared material was soon exhausted. This situation compelled the writer to continue working under exceptionally heavy pressure. Concomitantly he learned that his wife's illness was hopeless. She died on October 19, 1885 in Falkenstein and was buried in Warsaw.

Notwithstanding his severe trials, Sienkiewicz did not stop to work on *The Deluge*. Its final instalments were printed in August 1886. When the noted Danish critic Georg Brandes arrived in Warsaw for a series of lectures, Sienkiewicz made his acquaintance. He referred to this meeting in a humorous way, questioning the competence of the distinguished literary savant. In autumn, he left for Turkey in order to become more familiar with the oriental world, which he planned to introduce in the last part of the trilogy *Pan Wolodyjowski* (Pan Michael). He toured Istanbul where he visited the mosques and museums. There he met a Turkish diplomat, with whom he was able to discuss Polish-Turkish relations during the seventeenth century. His itinerary included a sojourn in Italy. On his return trip he stopped at Vienna and Cracow.

One of the habits which could hardly ease his literary activity was the author's nomadic way of life. He was fond of traveling in his younger years. Because of his wife's poor health, he was compelled to make trips for her sake. His liking for travel did not cease with her death. Even in Poland, he often went to the mountain resort of Zakopane and was a frequent guest at the spas of Krynica, Naleczow, and Szczawnica. On numerous occasions he made trips abroad to the fashionable resorts at Ostend, Teplitz, Karlsbad, Biarritz, and many others.

In the 1880's, the novelist's works began to be known abroad.

His tales appeared in Czech periodicals as early as in 1880. In America *The Catholic World* printed in 1884 a short story "Paul," which was a translation of the initial version of "From the Memoirs of a Poznan Tutor."[24] *Slowo* gave permission to publish a French translation of the *Trilogy* in 1887. This agreement was only formal in nature, as no copyright convention existed between Russia and France at that time. By 1890 Jeremiah Curtin had started to translate *With Fire and Sword* and soon made Sienkiewicz's works available to the English-speaking world.

The novelist began writing *Pan Michael* in April 1887. He was cognizant of the fact that his previous contracts with the newspapers where his novels were serialized had been unfavorable and took steps to correct this situation. He presented more demanding conditions to *Slowo,* and to his pleasant surprise they were accepted without objection. The reading public greeted the last part of the *Trilogy* ardently; Maria Konopnicka, the leading poet of that period, devoted a long, favorable review to its first volume as soon as it appeared.

Feeling unwell, the writer went to the health resorts in Gastein and Ostend, where he wrote "Ta trzecia" (The Third One), a tale displaying an infrequent gay mood. In September 1888, he journeyed to Spain where he spent forty days. It was his intention to produce a book based on his Spanish impressions, but the only literary result of this excursion was a sketch entitled "Walka bykow" (The Bullfight).

An anonymous donor sent Sienkiewicz a considerable sum of money (15,000 rubles) with a slip of paper containing the message "Michael Wolodyjowski—to Henryk Sienkiewicz." In an open letter in the press the author stated that the custom of presenting monetary gifts to writers and artists was quite common in the West, but that in Poland, where so much poverty existed, other needs were more pressing. Therefore, although he was grateful, he could not accept such a present. If the money was not called for within three years, it was to be used for some charitable purpose. The anonymous donor approved of the novelist's generosity, and Sienkiewicz established a special fund to assist artists threatened with tuberculosis, a disease he regarded as an almost personal enemy. In this manner the writer paid tribute to the memory of his beloved wife.[25]

Negotiations with the publishers regarding the new novel *Bez dogmatu* (Without Dogma) began in the winter of 1889. The author wrote his sister-in-law Jadwiga Janczewska that he wished to illustrate "what life would be without a dogma" and to depict a man with a skeptical mind, oversophisticated, lacking simplicity and deprived of moral principles.[26] He consulted Janczewska's opinion regarding sharply drawn or realistically presented sensual scenes; on the strength of her advice, he shortened an episode dealing with the romance of the protagonist and Mme Davies.

Sienkiewicz took an active part in the arrangements preceding the return of the ashes of Adam Mickiewicz, Poland's greatest Romantic poet, from the cemetery of Montmorency in Paris, France. In 1890 the remains of the author of *Pan Tadeusz* were exhumed and transferred to their final resting place in the Wawel Cathedral in Cracow, the Polish Westminster Abbey. At the end of the same year, the writer completed a short story called "Wyrok Zeusa" (The Verdict of Zeus) which revealed a budding interest in the ancient world.

In 1890 the novelist also embarked upon an expedition to Africa. He traveled there via Italy and spent New Year's Day (1891) in Cairo. Because he missed his ship, the writer stayed almost a month in Egypt and visited the cities of Alexandria, Suez, and Port Said. In February he left for the island of Zanzibar. Some time later, Sienkiewicz joined a safari into the heart of the African continent. He contracted malaria and was confined to a hospital. By the end of April, he was back in Cairo. Upon his return to Europe, he was obliged to continue medical treatment. He recorded his experience and observations in *Letters from Africa*.

During one of his stays abroad, Sienkiewicz met Maria Romanowska, a pretty young woman, and her foster mother Helena Wolodkowicz. The girl had some literary ability, and she began writing the author many long letters, usually with prostscripts by her guardian. Sienkiewicz expected this romantic affair would soon fade away. However, some obliging friends suggested marriage; and gradually the writer himself began to treat the affair more seriously and paid a visit to the Wolodkowicz family in Odessa. The trip was rather expensive, and he was short of funds at that time. This financial need was probably a contributing factor in Sienkiewicz's decision to write another novel with a contemporary setting, *Rodzina Polanieckich* (The Polaniecki Family).

The writer proposed marriage and he was accepted. Mrs. Wolodkowicz planned an elaborate wedding in Rome, but formal obstacles presented by Italian law became so disconcerting that she agreed to a ceremony in Cracow. The wedding was delayed and finally took place on November 11, 1894, with Cardinal Dunajewski officiating. At first the writer was elated, but very shortly things began to go wrong. By the end of December, Maria had abandoned her husband, leaving him a nervous wreck. Sometime later ecclesiastical authorities in Rome annulled the marriage.[27]

The *Polaniecki Family* was completed less than a month before the novelist's unhappy marriage. Then he became preoccupied with the plan of his new work *Quo Vadis?*. He perused the classical writers, studied the history of ancient Rome, and read numerous books treating the first century A.D. He made yet another excursion to Italy to visit the places he intended to use as locales in the episodes of his novel. The first chapter was probably written in February 1895.

Sienkiewicz's popularity in his own country was limited because of the high price of his books. To remedy this, Wawelberg, a Warsaw banker, suggested the publication of the *Trilogy* in a cheap edition and loaned the money needed for the cost of the printing. The price of the *Trilogy* was thereby reduced from fifteen rubles to three. The enterprise was a complete success.

After a brief rest, Sienkiewicz wrote a tale called "On the Bright Shore." However, for the twenty-fifth anniversary of his literary career the novelist wished to produce a monumental work. Toward the end of 1895, he began writing *The Teutonic Knights*. The events of the narrative were set in the late medieval period, and the subject required thorough preparatory research.

In 1898 Sienkiewicz advised postponing his own jubilee in order to devote himself wholeheartedly to the erection of a monument to Mickiewicz in Warsaw. The Organization Committee elected Sienkiewicz their vice-chairman. He engaged a Polish sculptor, Cyprian Godebski, to carve a model for the proposed statue. The monument was unveiled on Christmas Eve, 1898, the hundredth anniversary of the poet's birth. Sienkiewicz drafted a speech, which had to be approved by the Russian officials. But the police forbade any speeches, and the ceremony took place in silence.

Jeremiah Curtin, the American translator of the novelist, arrived in Warsaw for the Mickiewicz Centennial. He brought with him a de luxe edition of *Quo Vadis?* and reported that although a single copy cost twelve dollars, it was sold out and was to be reprinted. For the publication of his works by Little, Brown and Company of Boston, the Polish writer received 25,000 francs. As for the translator, Sienkiewicz's success netted him a small fortune.[28]

In order to concentrate on *The Teutonic Knights*, the author accepted the hospitality of his friend Bruno Abakanowicz, who was a prosperous businessman and owned a home on the island of Ploumanach in Brittany. Sienkiewicz went there with his young relative, Ignacy Chrzanowski, a future historian of Polish literature. The novelist would shut himself up in his room from eight-thirty in the morning till noon, when he would appear on the plaza pale, with beads of perspiration on his forehead. When Chrzanowski asked him what had exhausted him so much, the writer replied, "work on the simplicity of style."[29]

The writer was a frequent visitor to Zakopane, a mountain resort in southern Poland and a favorite gathering place for intellectuals and bohemians.[30] Here Leon Wyczolkowski painted his portrait, which is considered one of the best. Later Olga Boznanska, who belonged to the Impressionist school, executed another portrait. *The Teutonic Knights* was completed in 1900, and the writer's postponed jubilee was finally scheduled. The event almost became a national holiday. Donations for a Jubilee Gift, to which all circles of the community subscribed, exceeded 70,000 rubles. With this sum the organizers purchased a small estate, called Oblegorek, situated in a hilly district near Kielce.

Various cities honored the author of *Quo Vadis?* but the main festivities took place in Warsaw on December 22. Many expressions of admiration and homage came from abroad; associations of Polish emigrants sent their felicitations, and the Pope, who saw some early film shots of *Quo Vadis?*, conveyed his blessing. In Russia the leading dailies devoted special issues and editorials to his literary achievement. Illustrations of his works done by Polish artists were exhibited in various Russian cities. A display of the author's mementoes was organized to benefit charity. Laudatory greetings arrived from all parts of the globe, a deluge so great that it even annoyed the novelist. According to *Czas* (The Time), he was reputed to have said on one occasion, "I have had enough of China and Sienkiewicz."[31] Since September 1901, rumors began to circulate in the press that the Polish author was a candidate for the Nobel Prize.

Sienkiewicz's fame became so widespread at the beginning of the twentieth century that, even when he appeared in a private capacity, he drew attention. People in various countries wished to learn as much as possible about the author, and journalists did their best to satisfy this curiosity. Louis E. Van Norman, who wrote his impressions of the fifth centennial of the University of Cracow in *The Outlook*, focused special attention on the novelist:

In the ancient church of Panna Anna [sic!] where the degrees were being bestowed, sat a great company of local dignitaries and visiting delegations from all over the world. Count Stanislaw Tarnowski, rector of the University, in his flaming crimson and ermine, presided. At his right hand, in plain evening dress, stood President Gilman, of Johns Hopkins. He was responding to the address of welcome for the universities of America. Said he: "America thanks Poland for three great names: Copernicus, to whom the whole world is indebted; Kosciuszko, who spilled his blood for American independence; and Sienkiewicz, whose name is a household word in thousands of American homes, and who introduced Poland to the American people." The novelist, who was in the audience, arose and bowed, blushing consciously, and the audience fairly went wild. One of the gigantic sidemarshals, in slushed buff waistcoat and vermillion topped boots, who stood near the writer, fairly shouted in his enthusiasm. "That's it," he cried approvingly when I translated the speaker's words, "that's it. As long as Sienkiewicz lives —*Jeszcze Polska nie zginela*" (Poland is not yet lost).[32]

Sienkiewicz's opinion of the contemporary Modernist and Symbolist writers was unfavorable. He agreed in principle that new literary trends should differ from past tendencies. He remarked that even in churches people sing the hymn "Let the people of the Old Testament give way to the New Testament," and added, "As far as I am concerned, I am always ready to yield, on condition that the New Testament would be wise, not stupid, and more moral than the old one, more beautiful and salutary. Does this happen now? As to myself—veto, not as an old Whig belonging to an ancient camp but as a man who tries to judge things as objectively as possible. Wyspianski is only a cluster of confused thoughts, or rather not so much thoughts as cleverly expressed feelings modelled in a shape reminiscent of barbarian times, and Przybyszewski is a lunatic asylum."[33]

A man nurturing such views could not appreciate the young who were experimenting in literature. Sienkiewicz disliked them for excessive brutality and flagrant eroticism. He made his opinions public and thus provoked a violent reaction. His most formidable opponent was Stanislaw Brzozowski, a leading critic of the "Young Poland" movement. Besides, other novelists, particularly Zeromski, were now coming to the forefront. Nevertheless, Sienkiewicz still had many devotees who eagerly awaited his books. For some time he planned a historical novel on the Sobieski period, and his publishers imprudently advertised it. When their promises failed to materialize, his readers became furious. In order to placate them, the novelist had to release a few fragments of *Na polu chwaly* (On the Field of Glory), which was still being written.

Notwithstanding his personal tastes, Sienkiewicz was always ready to assist young artists in every possible way. He learned that Stanislaw Wyspianski's health was failing and that his friends applied to the Academy in Cracow on his behalf for a grant. As the money already had been assigned to someone else, the writer could not intervene. Instead, he wrote a kind and persuasive letter to a financial magnate in Warsaw asking him to purchase some of Wyspianski's paintings. After the dramatist's death, he paid tribute by writing an obituary portraying him as an artist who reconciled deep patriotism with sublime purity of thought and feeling.[34]

In 1904 the writer married Maria Babska, a distant relative, who was neither young nor very attractive but who was a kind, sensible, and tactful woman. Only the immediate members of the family attended the wedding. Although the marriage was a result of convenience rather than sentiment, it was successful; and the bride's care for her husband contributed greatly to Sienkiewicz's peace of mind.

The writer finished his historical novel *On the Field of Glory* in August 1905. A few months later he was awarded the Nobel Prize jointly with the Austrian authoress Bertha von Suttner, who wrote the pacifist novel *Die Waffen nieder* (Arms Down). Sienkiewicz went to Stockholm where he took part in the official banquet and delivered an address in French.

As Prussian cultural pressure increased, Sienkiewicz intervened on various occasions. He issued a pamphlet defending the Polish schoolchildren. He participated in an inquiry held by the Parisian *Le journal* comparing the policy of Great Britain toward the Boers of South Africa with the anti-Polish repressions in Prussia. When a London monthly, *The Contemporary Review,* published an anonymous article on the extirpation policy conducted by the Prussians, Sienkiewicz provided a preface. In 1906 he published an open letter to Wilhelm II, which was widely circulated abroad.

The following year the Prussian government prepared a bill on the compulsory dispossession of Polish landowners. It stated that the administration was authorized to buy Polish land at arbitrarily fixed prices. A Polish committee replied by an appeal addressed to all nations, organizations, institutions, and prominent individuals. Sienkiewicz signed the document. The protest included some loaded expressions, such as "crime against humanity," "barbarity," "shameful outrage," "the greatest iniquity and infamy in the history of the twentieth century." The message had widespread repercussions. In the United States, *The Outlook* not only reprinted its text in full but asked a German to represent the Prussian opinion. The editor, acting as an umpire, summarized this exchange of views and warmly supported the Polish cause.[35]

Despite his preoccupation with current problems, Sienkiewicz did not neglect belles-lettres. He published a few short stories,

"The Bellringer," "In the Fog," "The Wedding," "The Moonlight Sonata," and others. He disapproved of the upsurge of the revolutionary movement which revived the spirit of armed resistance but which in the writer's opinion undermined the Polish community. In the summer of 1907 he conceived the idea of a novel *Wiry* (Whirlpools); it was his intention to stress the failures and abuses caused by immature revolutionary brooding. It was serialized and appeared from March 1909 to April 1910.

Anniversaries provided the impetus for arousing patriotic feelings in the divided country, and the community exploited such occasions to stimulate the national spirit. The centennial of the birth of Juliusz Slowacki in 1909 was one such opportunity. The poet was rediscovered by the Symbolists, who succeeded in making him popular. Sienkiewicz inaugurated the solemn public celebrations. He attached much importance to the five-hundredth anniversary of the Battle of Grunwald (Tannenberg) the next year. He wrote a special article to commemorate this historic victory of the united Slavic and Lithuanian forces over the Teutonic Order (in 1410). On the occasion of the unveiling of the monuments of Kosciuszko and Pulaski in the United States, he sent a message to the Polish Americans.

During the first decade of the twentieth century, the novelist's works inspired many artists all over the world. The theater of Sarah Bernhardt in Paris presented a stage adaptation of *With Fire and Sword,* and all tickets were sold well in advance. The noted artist Jan Styka rekindled the interest of Parisians for *Quo Vadis?* by painting a panorama, which attracted not only individual spectators but also group visits. Two films, French and Italian, were based on *Quo Vadis?*. A dramatized version of *Quo Vadis?* was performed in New York. Henry Cain wrote a libretto based on the same novel, and Jean Nogues composed the music for the opera. It was performed in Nice and Paris and later in Vienna, where Sienkiewicz saw its twenty-fifth performance. Feliks Nowowiejski composed an oratorio to the novel, which enjoyed much success in Germany.

At the decline of his literary career, Sienkiewicz resolved to address himself to a new category of readers. He decided to write a book for children. The setting would be Africa, and the writer promised to apply the same seriousness and concentration to this novel as he did to his works for adults. In this way, he realized his early dreams of exotic adventures. The work was completed in June 1911.

Now Sienkiewicz turned to the Napoleonic Wars and the participation of Polish legions in them. He planned to make yet another trip to Italy to see the battlefields he wanted to describe. The writer finished the second part of *Legiony* (The Legions) in July 1914, but the work was still far from completed. Although he was not a young man, he labored with his usual zeal and determination; but in his letters he occasionally accused himself of laziness:

As to my novel, there is probably no greater idler than myself, as far as the start is concerned, and I would consider myself a lazy-bones if I did not write so many volumes, and if I did not admire my diligence once I begin working. This reminds me of Zagloba, who lingered at the beginning of the battle but once he was compelled to fight, he amazed the world with his determination.[36]

At the outbreak of World War I, he was at his estate in Oblegorek. Soon he came to the conclusion that it would be wise for him to settle in a neutral country, where his activity would be less restrained. He chose Switzerland and arrived there October 1914. The Poles organized two committees for relief of war victims in the Polish territories. One was located in Switzerland (with Paderewski as its guiding spirit), and the other was headquartered in Cracow. Both were apolitical and served only humanitarian purposes. However, Sienkiewicz realized that the Swiss Committee suggested some political implications as a reminder of the Polish nation and a hint to its intrinsic unity, which remained unimpaired despite the partitions. The novelist set to work for the Swiss Committee. A message to humanitarians on behalf of the Poles met with favorable response and brought in large sums of money.

Sienkiewicz objected to the politicians who made the Polish cause dependent upon the Central Powers, but he spoke with sympathy of the Polish young men serving in the Austrian Armed Forces. In an atmosphere of world conflict no time could be found for purely literary pursuits. *The Legions* was left in abeyance. The writer met the French author Romain Rolland, and this meeting provided an opportunity to discuss both current literary and political topics.

Since the belletrist was cut off from his native land, he was deprived of his usual sources of income. Fortunately, the French royalties for *Quo Vadis?* helped him to cover daily expenses. His seventieth birthday brought him a great number of greetings. For some time the author was kept busy writing notes of thanks. He secured the participation of Polish writers in the Shakespeare Memorial Book and contributed his own text to the volume. A short sketch entitled "Wspomnienie" (A Recollection) was Sienkiewicz's literary farewell; it was published posthumously in the Warsaw periodical *Tygodnik Ilustrowany* on November 25, 1916.

The writer suffered from sclerosis, and his health deteriorated rapidly. After a brief illness, he died in Vevey, Switzerland, on November 15, 1916. His funeral was organized by the Council of the Swiss Union, the representatives of the six Allied Powers, the delegates of the Serbian Academy and the Polish Associations in Switzerland. His remains were interred in the Roman Catholic cemetery in Vevey. Poles, though badly afflicted by the hardships of war, deeply mourned his passing. Expressions of grief in other European countries were severely hampered by military and political preoccupations.

The independent Polish Republic voted for the return of Sienkiewicz's remains to his native soil. On October 21, 1924, the coffin bearing the novelist's body left Vevey. In Lausanne, Fribourg, Bern, Zurich, Innsbruck, Vienna, as well as in cities in Czechoslovakia, representatives of government, dignitaries, intellectuals, and readers paid their last homage to the world-renowned author of *Quo Vadis?*. At the Polish frontier, the train was met by Polish delegations, and by way of Katowice and Czestochowa the coffin was transported to Warsaw, where it was placed in a separate vault in St. John's Cathedral. After 1945, Sienkiewicz was recognized as one of the twelve great Polish writers, whose literary heritage was placed under the patronage of the state.

CHAPTER 2

Journalistic Jaunts

I Apprenticeship

DURING his early literary career, Sienkiewicz wrote theater reviews and occasional topical essays. Five of his youthful narrative-fiction works attracted the attention of the public. However, the bulk of his output consisted of "chronicles." They were mainly regular reviews of current events, written in a light mood. This kind of writing enjoyed much popularity and was Sienkiewicz's main assignment as a journalist.

The "chronicles" were modeled after the French *feuilletons*, but they acquired a more serious meaning in Poland. Because of the restrictions imposed by the Russian administration on political, cultural, and even social activities, these "chronicles" served as a means of influencing public opinion in an unobtrusive but efficient way. In them, various problems of everyday life were brought to the public's attention. Since they were written to appeal to a wide circle of readers, the function of this genre was to instruct as well as to amuse. Anecdotes and witticisms made them palatable, and a frequent change of topics helped to avoid monotony. One of the masters of this genre was Boleslaw Prus, who performed the tedious duties of a weekly "chronicler" for several decades. Sienkiewicz admired Prus's skill and considered him superior even to the French publicists.[1]

Naturally, the first steps of Sienkiewicz as "chronicler" were reserved. He lacked the zeal of the protagonists of the Positivist school. His style bore traces of journalistic jargon. The writer combed the press to find themes and episodes suitable for this kind of writing. Now and then, he experienced some embarrassment, especially when, with the arrival of summer vacations, the pulse of city life slowed down:

. . . where there is no lottery, when everything possible has been said of the weather, of the level of water in the Vistula, of the difficult plight of a feuilletonist, of cholera, of the fountains for birds in the Saxon Garden—when all these subjects are exhausted like the wit of some humorous periodicals, like the patience of their readers, like the pockets of the tenants paying the double price for their apartments, only then can one use the last of the available resources—and write of the theatrical producers or the owners of the dwelling houses in Warsaw.[2]

Occasionally the author inserted a story to illustrate some point. One of them, he said, was taken from the American legends. It was a rather lengthy allegory about a gentleman named Commerce who had a daughter called Profit. She was plain and not a very virtuous creature. A suitor came with the obvious intent of asking for Miss Profit's hand. His name was Wit; he looked meager, and his attire was shabby, but he oozed cheerfulness and confidence. The parents of the maiden did not think highly of him, yet the girl liked the gentleman so they were married. Their child called Advertising grew to be a precocious young lady. She liked to boast and talk about herself and used a highly exaggerated style; she never spoke the truth even as a joke. She built a palace for herself on the back pages of the daily papers, which became her permament abode.[3]

Once Sienkiewicz spoke in a jocular tone of the severity of Sikorski, his editor at *Gazeta Polska,* who allegedly brutally pruned his lyrical outbursts and demanded facts. A legend circulated presenting the young writer as a victim of an arbitrary supervisor cutting out all the more vivid and original passages of his "chronicles" and leaving merely bare skeletons. The accusation was unkind. On the contrary, Sienkiewicz owed a debt to his more experienced colleagues who taught him many valuable lessons and assisted him in improving the quality of his writing.

After two years' experience, the writer's style acquired more flexibility. His journalese was polished into simplicity and precision. He also became adept at selecting material suitable for his specific vehicle of expression. When necessary, his diction became vigorous and impressive. In one of his "chronicles" printed in 1875, he inserted a fine description of a modern industrial establishment in Zyrardow, which at that time seemed a Positivists' dream:

What a factory! The halls are so spacious that when you stand at one end, you can hardly distinguish the faces of people at the other end. The huge, terrific steam monsters roar loudly and swing their iron arms with devilish dash, putting everything in motion. In the weaving hall thousands of larger and smaller wheels rotate on their axles with awful speed; everywhere there is din and clatter and such turmoil that you cannot even hear a single word. The walls of the building tremble. It seems that all these machines live and have souls and that some unintelligible fury has seized these iron monsters. You look at them and feel that at any moment something horrible will stretch out towards you, snatch you and throw you among those teeth, hooks and belts, shred your body in atoms, grind you and make of you a yard of linen. To get transformed into a towel—what an unpleasant change, to say nothing of other shapes if you are woven in a finer quality of linen.[4]

After a disastrous fire in Pultusk, Sienkiewicz visited the town and drew an impressive picture of the place. He described the inhabitants who were crushed by the magnitude of their misfortune. He witnessed the vain efforts of the firemen trying desperately to extinguish the flames and stressed the inadequacy of their equipment. In particular, he was struck by an unforgettable scene:

On the meadow everywhere flashed little lights swung by a feeble breeze. Here the Jews spent their Sabbath under the open sky. This solemn camping site was a weird and moving spectacle. On tables or simply on the ground twinkled brass candlesticks, the glow of which faded struggling with the last rays of dawn. The tables were empty, without the usual Sabbath meal. One saw all around the tearful praying faces raised towards the sky. There was silence; no usual chants and screams of prayers were heard. Obviously the awe shut the mouths of these people and they prayed only with a silence of despair, with their hunger of tomorrow and their prospective misery, as hard as a stone and as heavy as a stone.

O Adonai! Have mercy upon us![5]

Some satirical scenes from the life of high society pointed to other talents of the chronicler. He developed the skill of observation. His apprenticeship in editorial offices had not been in vain;

and although he accepted gladly another assignment, he admitted in one of his American letters: "Sometimes I feel nostalgic about this sad role of a gnomic chronicler, which I performed for several years as well as I could . . ."[6]

II *The American Experience*

In the 1870's, America stirred considerable interest among the Polish public. The Positivist publicists watched the speedy economic progress of the United States with admiration. It could serve as a model and an incentive for improving their native land. The growing political repressions under the Russian regime favored dreams of mass emigration. This idea became even more acute under the Prussian occupation, where economic conditions forced some people to emigrate. The names of Kosciuszko and Pulaski had established a sentimental bond with America as a legendary shelter of democracy and freedom.

The interest in America resulted in many translations of books about the United States. *American Notes* (1842) by Charles Dickens was translated into Polish in 1844. Sienkiewicz mentioned it along with *Democracy in America* by Alexis de Tocqueville in his American letters.[7] On the eve of his departure in 1876[8] two new books appeared, *A Journey across North America* by Olympia Audouard and *New York and the American Society* by L. Simonin. As to Polish writers, Julian Horain dispatched enthusiastic reports from California; Christine Narbutt published an account "In America"; Roger Lubienski printed his American correspondence in the weekly *Kronika Rodzinna;* and the gifted writer, Sygurd Wisniowski, discussed the abuses of the American administration and its politicians. A series of articles by Kalikst Wolski printed in the journal *Klosy* reappeared in 1876 as a book entitled *To America and in America.*[9]

Sienkiewicz gathered much material for his American letters from direct observation, and for some time he maintained the style of chronicler. However, his aim also was to present a general idea of the United States and to delineate the trends animating its society. On some occasions his Polish-American friends assisted him, but much of what he wrote was a result of study and reflection. He wrote separate essays on the Chinese in California and on the Polish settlements. Last but not least, he felt fascinated by the American countryside and portrayed many magnificent landscapes, which he saw on his trip across the continent and during his stay in California. As a result, his American letters had a threefold aspect: they were a reportage, a sociological study, and the idyllic memoir of an artist.

As many other Europeans, the author was at first shocked and disappointed by what he saw in America. Of the streets of New York, he said they were muddy, littered, and badly paved. Near the harbor he saw slums "a hundred times dirtier" than those of London. He wrote of the proletariat, white and Negro, consisting of the scum of various nations—ugly, emaciated, decimated by all kinds of disease. He felt sorry for the poor immigrants lacking the funds for a railroad ticket which might give them a chance of rural settlement; they stayed in the cities, doomed to idleness, cold, want, and starvation. On the other hand, he pointed out that the treasures accumulated on Wall Street would suffice for the purchase of entire countries. Sienkiewicz contrasted the 170 billion francs involved in the transactions of the New York banks and commercial houses with the recent war indemnity of 5 billion francs which the victorious Bismarck imposed on France, hoping to ruin it forever. In the novelist's eyes, the city was an accumulation of bankers, industrialists, and merchants engaged in business from early morning till night, impressive and dynamic on the surface but fundamentally boring, producing plenty of money, but lacking any other purpose.

The manners and customs of the average citizens jarred him. He missed the politeness of the European Continent. He observed that the American community enjoyed the opinion of a very religious society; but, being matter-of-fact, it did not concern itself with things having no immediate practical value, and hence was incapable of metaphysical reflection. People in America went to church on Sundays and read their Bible, but these habits were a mere routine lacking in genuine piousness.[10]

The initial disappointments did not discourage the traveler. Time and again, Sienkiewicz stressed that he wished to be impartial and accurate and that his critical remarks did not result from any preconceived dislike of American institutions. His training in the Positivist school of thinking had taught him that social organization was never good in an absolute sense, as its value depended on the character of a nation, its conditions, customs, and cultural inheritance. If any institution began to retard progress, it would become undesirable. Applying this theory to the United States, the writer considerably modified his early judgments. His resources were limited: he did not meet any outstanding American intellectuals and politicians and did not even visit the capital. He was guided by his instinct as an experienced newspaperman and by the reports of other travelers.

Of the various groups of immigrants, the writer singled out the Irish. In his opinion, their economic situation was relatively bad, but their role was beneficial for American society, as it helped to establish the desirable balance. "I see now," remarked the author, "my Positivist colleagues smiling; but I do not stop maintaining what I said. An excessive preponderance of an idealistic mood is harmful to society: it creates daydreaming, political Don Quixotism, hope for heavenly intervention. . . . This is an undeniable truth—but it is also true that every extreme is harmful."[11]

The writer noticed discrepancies and antagonisms among different ethnic groups. Nevertheless, he considered their amalgamation as the greatest American achievement. He praised the policy of a government which allowed each minority group to cultivate its own way of life so that assimilation proceeded smoothly:

According to me, America with its institutions and customs is a very instructive country. After all, one enormous social problem has been solved here. Forty million people from various nations, often mutually hostile in Europe, live here in accordance with the law, in harmony and freedom. Since everything in this world has some bad and good sides, liberty may also have its negative aspects. But in spite of these aspects, the sun of liberty still brings warmth and life. America proves that such institutions—their faults not withstanding—allow the development of all sorts of interest.[12]

Sienkiewicz did not seem to realize the importance of the Negro's plight, but he was aware of the maltreatment of the

American Indians. He spoke of them with compassion but without the zeal and indignation one would expect from a representative of an oppressed nation. He saw in their extinction the consequence of an implacable social law. The Indians could not adapt themselves to a new civilization (which they saw in its worst possible form) and consequently this civilization was driving them from their land, inexorably and brutally. Speaking of his encounters with the Indians, the novelist noted that they preserved some traditional practices which, however, lost their proper significance and in altered conditions became so meaningless that they often produced a pathetic effect.[13]

Sienkiewicz spoke of the corruption in the courts of justice arising from the election of magistrates who had no tenure and therefore exploited their term of office most ruthlessly. He condemned lynching, yet he judged even more severely a passive attitude and tolerance of abuses by the citizenry which he noticed in his own country. He emphasized that, in contrast to Europe, where it was impossible to take any action without some restrictive interference, self-reliance and dynamic ebullience flourished in America. He thought that American life was less refined but that it concealed enormous potentialities. Mixtures of various nations produced a fine race of men. The Yankee did not bother about details and trifles, but viewed the picture as a whole; in every situation he behaved like a tough, resolute fellow. "He knows how to love, but not how to knife you behind your back."[14] The writer believed that the American loved his country and was proud of it. In the hour of danger he would take his Kentucky rifle, roar like a bull, and stand united as one man with his fellow Americans.[15]

Sienkiewicz did not approve of the abuses of capitalism but came to admire American democracy. He said that in America every individual was encouraged to engage in any kind of occupation without fear of humiliation or loss of social position. A cab driver might enter the living room of a millionaire-rancher and entertain the host's daughter. A former general could run a saloon and personally serve beer and whiskey to his patrons.

Respect for labor enhanced equality. Knowledge possessed by Americans did not compare favorably with that of the European elite, and manners were not so elegant. But European civilization was confined to a limited circle of the upper class, which left the masses uncultured, ignorant, and reduced to purely physical needs. In the New Continent knowledge and good manners were less refined, but they belonged to the whole society. If civilization meant not an abstract value but promotion of happiness, its impact in America was greater than anywhere else. Three factors, respect for labor, relative equality of education, and lack of disparity in manners were, in Sienkiewicz's opinion, the mainstay of American life.[16]

American women thrilled the novelist, mainly because they were so different than their European counterparts. He devoted a separate letter to their charms. Their ostentatious and elaborate attire looked, in his eyes, especially strange alongside that of the men, who did not care about their clothes. He also remarked that the women had little appreciation for literature, the arts, or music; that they did not know any foreign languages; and that they they did not cultivate any special talents as was customary in most European countries. However, he emphasized the leading role of women in American public education. In the schools he visited the teachers conducted lessons while walking among the pupils, and adapted themselves to the individual child. The writer approved of teaching that started from the nearest objects and gradually progressed to a broader scope. Owing to the practical tendency in teaching, American children not only acquired the three R's but learned to understand politics as well. Sienkiewicz considered the huge sums of money spent on education a sound investment.

During his stay in California he became aware of an acute labor problem. Underprivileged Chinese immigrants provided cheap labor and found jobs more readily than whites; "in the conflict between capital and labor they tipped the scales decisively in favor of capital." The writer saw people preparing themselves for a massacre of the Chinese. Huge crowds marched bearing banners with such slogans as "Self-preservation is the first law of nature." The threat of slaughter did not materialize; the crowd sent a deputation to Congress, and they decided to boycott Chinese products.

Another letter depicted the Polish settlers, whose hardships later provided material for the short stories. The author emphasized the important role of the clergy but pointed out that they indulged in political activity and caused some disunity in their exclusion of Protestants who hailed mostly from western Poland. Nonetheless, the church helped keep the flock together. The writer dismissed the dreams of settling all Poles in a single state and the calling of a Sejm (parliament) as unrealistic. He felt that the Poles were worse off than other minorities. But Polish colonists contributed to American patience, endurance, and physical strength. They were accustomed to being content with little and could live without the conveniences other immigrants found indispensable. They were also sincerely attached to their new land. To the author their gradual assimilation seemed inevitable, and he did not believe they would preserve their native tongue.

His perception of America extended to nature as well as to sociological concerns. This passage on Nevada is an illustration of his descriptive technique:

Had Gustav Doré been born in America, I would say that he took the models for his landscapes of the inferno from the region through which we were now passing. Nothing oppresses the soul so heavily, nothing fills one with so much doubt and discouragement as these ridges of bare, black rocks. I imagine that this is the appearance of the dead ridges of the moon. Here, too, everything is dead. Nowhere is there a sign of vegetation; nowhere a single living creature. The rocks resemble tombstones; the plain one vast cemetery. This entire region seems to have fallen into a benumbed sleep as though bewitched by the spell of an evil spirit. A sense of fatigue adds to your depression and you feel that you, too, will succumb to sleep.[17]

Sienkiewicz was fascinated by the California landscape and called the land an earthly paradise. When he went with his host Max Neblung to the Santa Ana Mountains and stopped late at night with a squatter, Sienkiewicz forgot rest and food and immediately began to contemplate his new surroundings:

Black, piled-up masses of mountains enclosed the valley whose only outlet to the north and south was the bed of a deep mountain stream.

. . . Rocky cliffs hung over the valley in huge, titanic blocks, thrown up as if with confused fury one upon another. It seemed to me that at any moment these blocks might break loose and crash to the bottom of the valley. The bright night increased still further the extravagance of all these forms. The moon's beams threw a silver ribbon around the edges of the rocks whose black, motionless silhouettes were etched against the illuminated background with strangely severe clarity. The sounds of night heightened still more the grim spell of the environment. In the rock crevices covered with trees, wildcats wailed threateningly and hoarsely; now and again an owl hooted; at times the horses neighed.[18]

Powerful elements of nature impressed the writer with their eerie splendor. Occasionally, he succumbed to the spell of scenery which emanated sheer beauty reminiscent of the artful creations of human ingenuity:

This valley embracing about two square miles, was not so overgrown with dense and tangled vegetation as the others. It was, in fact, a Versailles garden in the wilderness, embellished with marvelous bouquets of trees and shrubs almost as though contrived by the hand of a gardener-artist. Dark, splendid groves of oak and small, attractively placed clumps of maple covered most of the region. Laurel bushes were set out in symmetrical beds. A row of trees created a kind of avenue which stretched beyond my sight. It was almost incredible that nature should have designed everything so artfully and harmoniously. A slight depression in the center of the valley was covered with grass of a bright, fresh greenness that betrayed the moistness of the soil. The tall shrubs there were completely hidden under the tangle of enormous wild grapevines.[19]

In his American letters Sienkiewicz was not profound, but he strove to be a fair reporter. He saw some bright spots, but he did not conceal the shades. For this reason various critics interpreted his general opinion of America in different ways. An isolated selection of critical remarks would sound like a severe condemnation; a shift to brighter observations would produce the opposite effect.[20] A solution to this dilemma was given in the letters Sienkiewicz wrote in Paris, soon after his return to Europe. At that time, he already looked upon his transatlantic adventures from a distance and was able to compare them with his new impressions.

III *View from France*

Vitality was the main feature attributed now by the novelist to the American nation. In France he traced the germs of decay reminiscent of the end of the declining Roman civilization. Time and again he returned to this analogy, and he even compared Paris with ancient Rome. The autocratic rule of Napoleon III left some deplorable traces and was partly responsible for the widespread corruption. The severe verdict was confirmed by contrasting the Americans and the French. Sienkiewicz believed that France could still regain her former position, but this would require the active participation of new social resources:

. . . Someone may ask: Is this a republic? Is this a democracy? But this is neither a republic nor a democracy. This is an unfinished banquet from the epoch of the last Nero. After a long Caesarean feast the roosters crow for the daybreak. Go to the outskirts of Paris; here the calm and dark city sleeps quietly—here sleeps the future Republic in order to resume tomorrow the work of revival with refreshed strength; go to the Champ de Mars, and instead of the echo of an orgy you will hear by day and night the resounding of hammers, the clatter of coaches, the whistling of locomotives—here French democracy is at work. It would be as wrong to judge Paris by its boulevards as all of France by Paris.[21]

Unfortunately, the French ruling classes were old and skeptical; their influence was detrimental to the best interests of the nation. Although the French thought of themselves as having a democratic society, their democracy differed radically from that in America:

I could say plenty of the French Republic, and particularly of French democracy. Both are far behind the Americans. Here they still declaim freedom—in America they live it. Here democracy exists in their heads, in America it has become a custom. In America the citizens and the government are the same—in France concentration of power prevails, while in America decentralization dominates on the largest possible scale. Here a bureaucracy exists, higher and lower civil servants, a whole hierarchy of them—in America there is no such hierarchy, no bureaucracy.[22]

As can be seen, Sienkiewicz applied to France the American

criteria as a model of democracy. However, he was not indifferent to the charms of Parisian life, and he devoted to it a number of impressive portrayals. His description of Paris on the day of an important horse race is one of the best passages he ever wrote as a reporter. The same can be said of the scenes in which he showed the Parisians living an exciting life. Such scenes anticipated the splendors of the Roman Empire in *Quo Vadis?*:

Perhaps a poet will someday describe "the Parisian nights" in Boccaccio's style and I can tell you without exaggeration that they are strange nights. The open stores and coffee houses pour streams of light on the pavements; in the shop windows there are satin, velvet, pearls, diamonds; the theaters play and sing; the gardens resound with music; the brilliant, fashionable, sumptuous crowds fill the boulevards; the camelia girls move around like erratic comets with fair braids and eyes shining like stars. And if you wish, there is everything: the rustle of silk, the fragrant intoxicating air, the young and beautiful faces, the faint glances, the half-open lips, the whispers, the warm breaths, the quickening of the excited pulse, the inebriation, the frenzy. To complete the picture, a half-drunk Nero should appear among the crowds, lights, streets, and columns in a carriage drawn by tigers and the crowds should welcome him shouting "Ave, Caesar dive!"[23]

Sienkiewicz also highly appreciated the French theater and wrote with admiration of Sarah Bernhardt, the French actress whose supremacy at that time was unquestioned. Her portrait was another example of the writer's craft:

In "Hernani" I saw Sarah Bernhardt, the leading actress of today. She is not only a theatrical star, of whom all France is proud but also the most eccentric woman. She paints, carves, plays, writes poetry, sleeps in a room with the walls covered with a black shroud, a coffin for her bed; she is awaiting her death and is dying and while dying, she falls in love. She is eccentric, a little sick, tired and twisted but is an extraordinary character. As Doña Sol, she engraved herself for a long time in my memory. She is a slim, ethereal figure with a small tiny face, dreamy eyes and golden hair. Her Doña Sol is a pure maiden who fell in love with an eagle. However, the genius of Sarah Bernhardt does not reach the heights of such actresses as Rachel, Ristori, and Modjeska. In moments of pain and ecstasy of terror her voice turns into a scream and loses its pure tones; her outbursts are the outbursts of nerves, not impulses of inspiration. She is only a dove, not a dove and an archangel at the same time; finally she is always a little of Sarah Bernhardt, not the complete vivid character which she represents.[24]

IV *African Notes*

Sienkiewicz visited America and France as a journalist whose literary reputation was not yet fully established. He went to Africa as a recognized author. At first, he did not make any detailed plan of his trip, and as late as September 1890, four months before his departure a weekly reported that he intended to travel to Egypt.[25] On the other hand, he acquired references from various influential personages, e.g., Lord Robert Arthur Salisbury, Cardinal Lavigerie, Count Bertelli Algarotti, and others. In those days it was impossible to choose an independent route or to mix freely with the local population. This forced the writer to rely on indirect information, particularly in political matters.

His own experiences prejudiced him against the Arabs. "I like the black people very much but I cannot endure the Arabs," he wrote to a Polish friend.[26] He believed that the white administration was a blessing for the Negroes, as it safeguarded them from Arab abuses. From the humane point of view, he attached high priority to the liberation of the Negroes from the Arab slavemongers. It should be stated that Sienkiewicz saw only the eastern part of Africa, which as yet did not belong to the colonial system established by the European powers in other parts of the continent.

Only the first letter was written in Africa; the remaining ones were composed after his return to Europe. Even if he relied on some notes, one must concede that his memory was admirable. The African letters lacked the passionate curiosity that animated his American letters or the morbid fascination apparent in some of his French letters. Readers who expected adventurous tales were disappointed. On the other hand, the author displayed greater maturity and self-composure in these letters; now he was a master of diction and shunned melodrama. Still descriptive passages were the best parts of the African letters.

Of all his foreign travels, his stay in America left the most lasting impression on Sienkiewicz's mind. He saw a nation confronting many difficulties but remaining optimistic. Aware of American natural resources, he nonetheless attributed its successes to the courage, endurance, and faith of its people. Comparing these observations with the position of his own country, he at first cited its weaknesses but soon turned to the sources of strength and vitality, the only guarantees of survival and of ultimate triumph.

"Letters from America" as well as "Letters from Africa" as literary genre differed from ordinary correspondence.[27] The author wrote the impressions of his two major trips abroad with the obvious intent of publishing them. The title "letters" was convenient as it did not hamper the writer with definite structural requirements. It could appeal to a wider circle of readers than the appellations "essays" or "sketches." In his letters, Sienkiewicz could deliver general reflections, descriptions, and more intimate impressions. The accumulation of these divergent trends contributed to the versatility and entertaining value of these sketches. They provided a suitable vehicle for displaying different aspects of literary skill and a valuable test on the eve of Sienkiewicz's major literary ventures. His American impressions refreshed the writer's fondness for adventure and were helpful in shaping the plots, heroes, and even the landscapes of the *Trilogy*. The French observations provided a stimulus for the description of a decaying Roman Empire ruled by a corrupt tyrant. As to his African sojourn, it became a nucleus of the author's future novel for youth, *In Desert and Wilderness*.

CHAPTER 3

Tales and Miniatures

I *The Early Sparring*

ALTHOUGH Sienkiewicz owed his fame mainly to his major novels, he continued to write minor works of fiction throughout his career. He wrote novelettes, tales, short stories, legends, and fairy tales. These works faithfully reflected different stages in the author's views and in the development of his craftsmanship. Some of them have appeared in short story collections.[1]

The early novel, *In Vain*, was mainly a reminiscence of the author's student life. Its complicated plot and sketchy characterizations deprived it of literary significance. As a reflection of the Positivist tendencies, one of the characters was called Szwarc, his foreign name pointing to his plebeian origin. Son of a blacksmith, Szwarc studied hard and succeeded in becoming a physician. Besides an education, he possessed other qualities usually attributed to the gentry, such as courage and generosity. A girl from an aristocratic family fell in love with him, which, of course, was a reversal of the habitual treatment of the Romantic motif.

A similar character appeared in the tale "Nobody Is a Prophet in His Own Country" printed in the volume *Humoresques from Worszyllo's Portfolio.* Having graduated from the University, Wilk Garbowiecki decided to start "organic work." He settled in a provincial district and purchased a little estate to which he applied the most modern methods of husbandry, thus introducing various improvements. He established a library, which he supplied with valuable books, taught his plowboys to read, and struggled against the inertia of the local community. His efforts to lead others, except for making his own estate a model, were ineffectual. The local gentry found his conduct alarming and even dangerous and raised a campaign against him. A bored local girl flirted with him, but when he proposed, she unceremoniously rejected him. A contrived, brutal provocation compelled him into a duel in which he was killed.

The hero was a mere embodiment of the ideals expounded by the Positivist publicists. Wilk's defeat did not mean that he was wrong but simply that he acted too recklessly, underestimating the obstacles he had to overcome. More realistic were the satirical sketches of the different provincial figures. The narrator, Worszyllo, was a staunch opponent of the young madcaps who told the story of Wilk as a warning. This added an ironic twist to the tale.

"The Two Roads," another story from the same collection, was also directed against the gentry. Despite the opposition of the local peasants, a frivolous squire ruined his estate and sold it to German colonists. The author ridiculed the shallow life of the drawing rooms, where the gentry aped English manners and where snobbery and pretense predominated. The rival of the squire, an educated engineer, was simply the prosperous owner of a factory. The girl whom both men wanted to marry did not hesitate to choose the commoner, rejecting the squire.

These early tales, with an obtrusive social message, were much like those of other contemporary authors. The Positivist heroes were a crop of wishful thinking rather than a product of real life. Simplification of intricate social conflicts and an obviously contrived plot were the inevitable results.

The three remaining tales written by Sienkiewicz between 1875 and 1877 were so closely connected that some critics have designated them as "a little trilogy." The author drew from his youthful experiences for material; he even revealed to his translator J. Curtin that "Hania" was more or less his own personal story.

"The Old Servant" was a portrait of an elderly man attached to a manor. He was treated more a friend of the family than a servant. Sometimes he indulged in grumbling even when he received orders from his master. Being imbued with a military tradition, he taught the boys, the local priest, and even his granddaughter Hania military drill. He related fantastic tales about his exploits, which intrigued the children. Once he beat a German who berated his master, and he suffered a beating in return; when he was scolded for taking part in a brawl, he did not even try to justify his behavior.

"Hania" centered around his granddaughter who became a very attractive girl. Henryk fell in love with her; but she preferred Selim, a youth of Tatar descent, and eloped with him. Henryk defended her honor and fought with Selim. The love affair ended unhappily when the girl fell ill with smallpox and after her recovery became a nun. The duel as the only acceptable exhibition of honor and gallantry was an obvious climax. Henryk lovingly described his preparation for combat:

I carefully wiped the sabre with soft cottonwool; on its wide blue blade, in spite of some 200 years, not even the slightest blemish was visible, although in its day it cut enough helmets and epaulettes, drank enough Swedish, Tatar, and Turkish blood. The golden inscription "Jesus, Maria" shone distinctly; I tried the edge, it was as sharp as the edge of a satin ribbon. The blue turquoises on the hilt seemed to smile as if begging for a hand to grasp it and warm it up.[2]

The last tale, "Selim Mirza," was intended as a narrative of the Polish Insurrection of 1863, but instead the author linked his heroes with the Franco-Prussian War. Selim distinguished himself in guerrilla warfare and experienced some unusual adventures; the oddest one was a clash between the Germans and the fugitives escaping in a balloon, which lost gas and dragged on the ground. Here the fascination of the author with adventurous elements was given prominence and anticipated his subsequent historical novels.

"The Charcoal Sketches" (1876) touched upon one of the dangerous by-products of the peasant emancipation. The free peasants at times needed advice and guidance, particularly in legal matters. Annoyed by petty squabbles, the squires avoided interference in peasant affairs. The bailiffs and aldermen, who usually lacked education, were unacquainted with the laws and regulations. They, in turn, had to rely on some secretary, often a man without scruples in a powerful position. What was the lot of a poor peasant who found himself in trouble?

In a typical village called Ram's Head, the Secretary, a vulgar, corrupt official, was dictator of the entire administration. He wooed the pretty wife of a peasant, and, when she drove him away, he applied blackmail. For fifty rubles, the woman's intoxicated husband signed a paper; when he regained his senses, he learned that he had signed an agreement to serve in the Russian Army. As head of the family, he was legally free of this obligation and hence the contract was invalid. Unaware of this, he became panic stricken.

When he confided his plight to his wife, she took the initiative into her own hands. The local court did not help the couple and even arrested the husband. The parson was too senile to be of use, and his young assistant piously advised the woman to offer all her troubles to God. The squire's daughter directed her to her father, who presently washed his hands of the whole affair; he sent the woman to the nearest town where she was incapable of properly explaining her case. When the Jewish innkeeper who knew all the local secrets told her that everything depended on the Secretary, the desperate victim turned to the villain. She confessed her sin to her husband, who murdered her and set fire to the squire's farm buildings. The narrative introduced a gallery of typical figures of country life. The writer drew their silhouettes in a cool, detached way, showing a series of simple but expressive scenes. The grim finale came as an inevitable, logical conclusion. There was no sentimental note in the story; the author maintained an ironic distance to the very end.

"Yanko the Musician" (1878) emerged from another anxiety of the Positivists—waste of peasant talent due to lack of education. Other writers usually stressed technical abilities. In his short story "Antek" Boleslaw Prus introduced a peasant lad who wanted to build windmills.[3] As late as 1889, Orzeszkowa in her novel *Nad Niemnem* (On the Banks of the Niemen) depicted a violinist and painter as mere parasites, while a pianist married a farmer and found happiness in everyday practical work.

Sienkiewicz's Yanko possessed all the rudiments of a promising musical genius. Nature appealed to him through sound. The only music he ever heard was in the church or from the tavern. Yet, this undernourished, ten-year-old boy was attracted to any music by an irresistible power. He made himself a violin of shingle and horse hair, but its sounds were weak. He once caught sight of the butler's violin in the manor, and from that moment on he dreamed of it. One night he entered the dining room hoping just to touch the instrument. He was caught, suspected of theft and punished. The beating was so severe that the frail child died.

The plot was simple but was strengthened by the stress of the mood which permeated the narrative. Sienkiewicz described in detail the budding musician, intensifying the mood with occasional ironic touches. He attributed to the members of the local court of justice a feeling of compassion for the little culprit.[4] Indeed, nobody intended to be cruel, but the child did not survive the excess of grace granted him. The writer painstakingly elaborated on the image of the dying boy whose last moments still reflected the only passion in his drab life.

Another ironic twist appeared in the finale. In the manor two young people conversed about their recent Italian trip. The gentleman grew enthusiastic over Italy as a country of artists, while the young lady spoke of the happiness of discovering these talents and assisting them. A single sentence followed: "Birches rustled over Yanko's grave."

The studied diction of the author's own speech was at variance with the simplicity of the content, but the story produced a powerful though melodramatic effect. Besides having been translated into many languages, it recently gained an unexpected resonance in a fine Mexican film, *Yanco,* which won prizes at sixteen international film festivals. The producer, Servando Gonzales, incorporated the plot of the tale adapting it to a Mexican locale. The boy was called Juanito, and "Yanco" became the name of the fiddle which he received from a former famous violinist.

In "Jamiol" (1878, a peasant corruption of the word *aniol* meaning angel) the Positivist tendency was still present but less obvious. Once more the narrative referred to the lot of peasant children. Marysia's mother died. After attending the funeral, the orphan remained with some women of the village in church. The ladies attended the vespers, sang a few hymns, and then went to the local tavern for solace. After a few drinks one of them, feeling sorry for the girl, said to her, "Remember, little orphan, what the parson told you when people were covering your mommie with snow that an angel watches over you." A man came to bring the girl to the squire's manor, and he too had been drinking. In the forest he overturned the carriage in a ditch and fell asleep. The child failed to awaken him and left alone. The snow was deep; Marysia soon grew tired and sat under a tree to rest, hoping that the guardian angel would take care of her.

Indeed someone approaches; although the snow is soft, it rustles distinctly; someone's steps are nearer and nearer, still but swift. The child raises with confidence her sleepy eyelids. What is this? Some gray triangular head with protruding eyes observes the child carefully . . . horrible . . . abominable . . .[5]

The author pointed out distinctly who was really responsible for the accident. The local squire wrote an exhaustive article in which he demonstrated that the right of the manors to distil brandy was a foundation of social structure: in winter, vodka warmed people up and was their only consolation; therefore, attempts to deprive the landlords of the exclusive right of distilling it were harmful to the community. The story owed its weird effect to the accumulated contrasts of the dusky church, where a banner depicted sinners in the company of devils surrounded by flames, with the bright, noisy atmosphere of the tavern with its brash hurdy-gurdy.

II *Home and Abroad*

The title "From the Memoirs of a Poznan Tutor" suggested a connection with the Prussian partition, but actually the initial version of this tale took place under the Russian yoke. When the author decided to publish it in Warsaw, he had to change the locale because of censorship. The first text had appeared in *Gazeta Lwowska* in 1879, signed with three *x*'s, and for several decades the author remained unknown. Yet the secret was not respected in the United States, as the original anti-Russian version translated into English and printed in the *Catholic Review* in 1884 was signed with Sienkiewicz's full name as well as his literary pseudonym "Litwos."

It was the story of Michas (Paul in the first English translation), a normal boy who could not meet the requirements of his schoolteachers. He did his utmost to please both them and his widowed mother. The tutor, the narrator of the story, treated the child with sympathy and understanding and tried to assist him in the best possible way. Michas occasionally received a few good grades but eventually broke down under the strain. Dismissed from school, he contracted brain fever and died.

What were the reasons for his failure? Pupils had to memorize huge quantities of abstract encyclopedic data. Too much homework made relaxation after school hours virtually impossible; and there were examinations. Difficulties mounted because of the language barrier, as the instructors spoke exclusively German. The boy frankly confessed to his tutor that at times he didn't know the answers; however, more frequently he knew them but could not find the proper words to form a reply. His teachers ridiculed Poland, its history and culture—everything that the boy respected and loved; many times he returned home deeply disturbed. If he inadvertently uttered a Polish word during a conversation with his classmates, he was reprimanded. The German teachers regarded him as a child infected with dangerous principles and evil instincts.

The author handled his theme with moderation, avoiding an excess of melodrama. He reduced the background to a few essential details. A hint revealed that the boy's mother was victimized for her patriotism. As for the tutor, his hopeless love for Michas' mother remained a secret which he never disclosed. In the second version of the story, this motif was pruned to a minimum.[6]

"Bartek the Conqueror" presented another anxiety connected with western Poland. After the victorious wars with Austria and France, Prussian oppression increased. Sienkiewicz wished to shed light on the causes of the political setbacks suffered by the local population and to clarify the social responsibility for the blunders.[7]

Bartek Slowik, who was a typical Polish peasant, disliked and distrusted the Germans. However, when he was called into the Prussian Army, he fought against the French like a lion, not only in self-defense, but because he thought they were Germans, only worse. Once he had the opportunity to liberate some Poles taken prisoners, but his habit of blind obedience prevailed, and he missed his chance. He received many decorations for gallantry and proudly returned to his native village. He soon found that the Prussians treated his son and himself with spite and scorn. He was involved in a brawl, and the court put him in prison. His wife had to borrow money from a Prussian neighbor to cover the costs of legal proceedings. They were later unable to repay it. The local squire was willing to help, but changed his mind when he learned that Bartek, terrorized by the local magistrate, voted for a German candidate for parliament. The hero from Sedan was treated by his own countrymen as a traitor. His land was sold at auction, and the penniless Bartek was forced to leave with his family for the city. There he still had to go to prison.

Journalists from the western provinces raised some objections. They accused the author of not knowing the real peasants of their region. These criticisms were not quite justified, as the writer's central character was based on a generalized model of the peasant viewed as a mainstay of national revival. This broadened the scope of the story and made the situation applicable to the other two parts of occupied Poland.

Under proper circumstances, Bartek could have become a definite asset; but due to his lack of education he succeeded only in being an advantage to his enemies. The situation might have been different if the peasants had found leadership or guidance among the Polish landlords who were better educated. The lack of understanding on the part of the squire and the pressure to which Bartek was subjected was the crux of the matter. Having lost the election, the squire simply left for Dresden, abandoning his peasant neighbors to their fate.

The tale was colored with sardonic irony. In spite of some discrepancy with the actual background, it produced a powerful effect. As late as 1914, the German authorities forbade its dissemination. All copies sold publicly or offered for sale, as well as the printing plates, were to be destroyed. To justify this censorship, the order pointed out that such works incited the

Polish population against the Germans.[8] Despite its sad ending, the story conveyed a constructive message. The emphasis on vitality and the call for more enlightenment were not lost on the readers.

In the 1870's, the Prussians intensified their efforts to buy land from the Polish owners. Although the action ultimately failed, it first brought some successes to the Prussian administration. The peasants suffered various setbacks, and some moved to the cities; others emigrated to America, lured by false promises of unscrupulous agents.

In his American letter on the Polish settlements in the United States the author discussed various aspects of Polish emigration. The main facts mentioned by the writer were almost identical with those in the story "After Bread" except that the final conclusion was more cheerful: the settlers had to experience many drawbacks, but they eventually adapted themselves to their new environment.[9] As to the tale, it was written as a deterrent, and Sienkiewicz conceived it as a lecture which was given repeatedly in 1880.

The story did not attribute the emigration directly to the political conditions. Toporek had a dispute with his neighbor and lost his case in court. In addition, the harvest was bad. In a moment of depression, a cunning agent arrived and lured the peasant with visions of the paradise that awaited him on the other side of the ocean. Toporek sold his farm and sailed to the United States with his only daughter Marysia. They suffered painful hardships and perished.

"After Bread" was melodramatic in tone. But in order to assess it justly, one should bear in mind that it was addressed to a specific kind of listener and reader and that it was meant to serve a definite purpose—to discourage potential emigrants.

The pathetic mood should not overshadow the realistic aspect of the story. The deceitful lies of the agents preying upon the naïve peasants; the helplessness of the newcomers completely unprepared to cope with a foreign way of life; the scenes of everyday life in the obscure districts of New York; the misfortunes of the settlers—all these episodes reflected real situations.

The story aroused the interest not only of the Poles, but also of other communities from which the prospective immigrants were recruited.

"Lillian Morris" (original title: "Przez stepy," Across the Plains, 1878) was an idyllic story of love between a sweet American girl and the Polish captain of an immigrant party. The wagon train drove to California during the gold rush. Their journey was full of misfortunes, and the girl could not endure the trials. The story anticipated the escapes in the *Trilogy,* and the landscapes were a foretaste of the Ukrainian scenery.[10]

"The Lighthouse Keeper of Aspinwall" was also related to Sienkiewicz's stay in America. The inspiration for the story came from a reminiscence of a Polish emigrant of whom the novelist wrote briefly in one of his letters from California.[11] Skawinski, the protagonist of the story, was a political exile. He worked at all kinds of jobs. He was a gold digger in Australia, a diamond seeker in Africa, a rifleman in India. The drought frustrated his attempts at farming in California. He went to Brazil to start trading with the aborigines, but his raft was wrecked on the Amazon River.

The wanderer became tired and lost hope of ever finding a peaceful abode. At last he was hired as a lighthouse keeper on a small, isolated island, where no one bothered him; and he could enjoy the peace of mind he had lacked for so many years. People at the seashore respected him. On Sundays, he would leave his refuge to attend church services but promptly returned after Mass as if he distrusted the mainland. He hoped to spend the rest of his days in his solitary tower.

One day Skawinski received a parcel containing a book. It was the epic poem of Mickiewicz, *Pan Tadeusz.* The old man began to read it. By the magic of poetry his native land appeared before his eyes in its splendor and beauty. He spent the whole night in a reverie. Early in the morning he learned that he had forgotten to kindle the light and was responsible for a shipwreck. Once again he had to resume his nomadic life. He left the island more destitute than ever, but his eyes shone, for he carried the book with him; it was now his most precious possession.

[*68*]

Tales and Miniatures

This tale encompasses the condensed history of the life of a wandering exile. The essential details are supplied with laconic precision, making the story moving without sentimentality, and pathetic without rhetorics. From the structural point of view, it is one of the best stories ever written by Sienkiewicz. The climax, which is at the same time surprising and natural, was prepared with expert skill. A distant historical perspective, discreetly suggested, enriched the fabric and showed the wide possibilities of the short story as a literary species.

"Wspomnienie z Maripozy" (Memories of Mariposa) was devised as a loose report on a visit to a former boom town. After the gold rush, this town was reduced to one-tenth of its original size. The most striking episode is the narrator's meeting with the Polish squatter Putrament, who had lived for over twenty years in Mariposa without contact with his countrymen. The squatter spoke Polish that surprised the visitor; it was the language of the sixteenth century, and sounded archaic and solemn. The guest's initial amusement ceased when he discovered that the host had only one Polish book, the Wujek translation of the Bible (1599), which he read daily in order not to forget his native tongue. The story contained no plot, and its main effect depended on a linguistic device. There was a parallel motif of a German who did not know Polish; but, being a former soldier of General Mieroslawski, he showed respectful admiration for his former commander by repeating such words as *freedom, progress,* and *civilization* whenever he spoke of him. In this way, two aspects were blended: the miseries of the exiles and the positive impact of their mission.

"Sachem," written in 1883, had to do with a settlement named Antelope which was built on the former Indian site Chiavatta, the capital of the Black Snakes tribe. One night the white squatters invaded this Indian territory and mercilessly killed off the unarmed natives. In the same place where they had hanged their victims, the colonists erected a church and a philanthropic institution; their pastors taught people the sacred law of love for all fellow men and respect for other people's property.

An itinerant circus arrived, and a large crowd gathered to see the performance. The main attraction on the program, which the public awaited with anxiety, was the appearance of an acrobat who supposedly was the only descendant of the chieftain of the Black Snakes! When he appeared in the arena, his face seemed hammered out of copper. He wore the traditional Indian attire and was heavily armed; he looked so dreadful that fear crept into the hearts of the spectators. The Indian started to walk along the wire. As he approached its end, he chanted a war song calling for revenge. The townspeople still remembered their encounter with the Black Snakes and recognized this awesome chant. When the tension had reached its peak, the warrior disappeared. Presently he returned with a metal plate, which he stretched toward the public in an imploring manner. At last, the audience felt relaxed and poured in their dollars and half-dollars.

To the uninitiated reader, "Sachem" sounded like a purely American tale, but the author addressed it first of all to his fellow countrymen. He reproved them for forgetting their former glories and for reconciling themselves to the shame and humiliation of slavery. He protested opportunism and called for the restoration of national dignity.

Other American stories reflected a lighter mood. The adventures of Orso, a circus athlete, anticipated some episodes in *Quo Vadis?*. The association of a strong man and a tiny girl in need of protection, which had appeared also in "Lillian Morris," would return in the *Trilogy;* in the fate of Ursus and Lygia; in Zbyszko and Danusia in *The Teutonic Knights;* and in the two heroes of *In Desert and Wilderness.* "The Comedy of Errors" exploited in a humorous way the confusion which arose when national groups in the American "melting pot" were compelled to live together.

III *Among the Bohemians*

In a few tales a more personal aspect prevailed. They raised the problem of the social standing of artists and intellectuals. Strangely enough, the atmosphere of these tales ranged from carefree gaiety to gloomy pessimism.

"The Third One" (1888) had all the ingredients of a farce.

However, the amusing entanglements served to illustrate a serious point as well. The author adopted an indulgent attitude toward artists to whom ordinary standards of behavior were difficult to apply. They stood apart from the bourgeois and the snobs. When they violated accepted conventions they followed an urge which was essential to their creative work. Sienkiewicz seemed to recognize the independence of art and to sympathize with the bohemians. In this respect, he was closer to the younger writers than to his own sober bourgeois contemporaries.

The representatives of "respectable" professions were shown in a satirical light. The author ridiculed the manners of high society, created a parody of the phraseology of polite conversations, poked fun at the rituals of social gatherings, and exposed the widespread ignorance of the arts. He singled out people who treated artists with scorn but began to adulate them as soon as they earned success. He derided journalists who supported unknown talents only when it was in the interests of their newspapers.

"Lux in Tenebris Lucet" (1891) introduced a sculptor, Kamionka, so destitute that he had to sleep in his studio. He lived in complete solitude as his friends abandoned him because of his ever increasing sadness. In his portrayal some resemblance to the author after the loss of his beloved wife could be suspected.[12]

Kamionka grew very weak, and the servant woman, his sole visitor, advised him to engage a sister of charity, who would take care of him without charge. When she left, the candle soon burned out, and darkness enveloped the studio. Presently, the pale light shone in through the venetian window and the sculptor saw a sister of charity. In her he recognized his late wife, and he announced that he was ready to die. She just smiled and pointing downward said,

"Thou art dead already. Look!" He looked in the direction of her hand, and behold, under their feet he saw through the window in the ceiling of his gloomy and lonely studio that here on the bed lay his own corpse with its mouth wide open, which in its yellow face seemed a dark hole, as it were. And he looked at that emaciated body as something foreign. But after awhile all began to vanish from his eyes, for that surrounding brightness as if urged by the wind from beyond this world, went off somewhere into infinity.[13]

This epilogue introduced a unique element previously not present in Sienkiewicz's works. Usually he wrote realistically and avoided supernatural intrusion. In this exceptional instance he deviated from this principle and approached the Symbolists.

The problem of bohemian artists reappeared in a different social setting in the short story "Organista z Ponikly" (The Organist from Ponikla, 1893). Klen was a musician whose talent was much appreciated, yet he suffered great poverty. Nevertheless, he persisted in his vocation. When at last luck smiled at him, he froze to death while returning from his fiancée's. Misfortune seemed to be the frequent lot of Sienkiewicz's artists.

IV Search for Light

In later years the author turned to stories in which the symbolic or allegorical meaning overshadowed human problems. "Pojdzmy za Nim" (Let Us Follow Him, 1892) gained fantastic acclaim. In the United States alone, it was reprinted about thirty times as a separate booklet and in anthologies. It owed its popularity to its optimistic view; and it foreshadowed the famous *Quo Vadis?*.

The basic ideas of *Quo Vadis?*—the critical appraisal of Rome and its ancient philosophy, and the moral victory of the new religion—were demonstrated in this story with purposeful simplicity. However, the magnitude of such a theme exceeded the scope of the short story form. For the author, it was a test case, indicating that for his new ideas he had to resort to the novel as a more suitable genre.

Occasionally Sienkiewicz added to his stories a touch of mythology and of Hindu lore. The legend "Be Thou Blessed" related the creation of a woman by Krishna, eighth avatar of Vishnu, and his decision that this beautiful and tender creature should seek refuge in the heart of a poet. "Dwie laki" (translated as "A Hindoo Legend") developed the author's design to show Death as irresistibly tempting, so that in order to keep mankind alive Vishnu had to create the two monsters, Suffering and Terror, to bar access to the bliss of eternal sleep.

The symbolic tales drew less attention from Polish readers than the earlier realistic stories. These tales were overshadowed by the vigorous production of younger writers. Abroad they found a warmer reception. Curtin collected several legends in a separate volume, of which a reviewer wrote with respect and enthusiasm.[14] Some legends were also reprinted in American periodicals as representative specimens of "the brilliant work" of the famous author of *Quo Vadis?*.[15]

Occasionally, the writer regained the crisp, ironic humor of his early tales. After the revolutionary upsurge of 1905, the relaxation of Russian censorship permitted the sharpening of critical sallies. Sienkiewicz's satirical vein was at its best in "The Judgment of Osiris" in which Egyptian trappings served as a transparent cover. The almighty Osiris was to pronounce a verdict on the soul of the deceased Egyptian minister Psunabudes (a grotesque name which may be rendered as Gone-to-the-doggies). The two immortal apparitions, Wickedness and Stupidity, tried to prove their right to priority. Both opponents threw on the scales heavy arguments substantiating their respective claims. However, neither could win, for it was impossible to find out whether the minister was more wicked or more stupid. Finally, the dignitary had to return to Earth in order to perform new deeds which would make the sentence feasible. "The Wedding" was written in the same vein, but its cutting edge was aimed at the author's own countrymen.[16]

* * *

In the early period of his literary career, Sienkiewicz vacillated between a longer narrative form, sometimes approaching a short novel or an extended tale ("Nobody is a Prophet Among His Own People," "Hania," "Lillian Morris," "After Bread," "Charcoal Sketches," "Bartek the Conqueror") and a regular short story.[17] As soon as the novelist began work on his *Trilogy*, he rarely returned to this intermediate literary genre ("The Third One," "On the Bright Shore").

The author did not treat his shorter works as a mere display of craftsmanship. Prior to 1883, he utilized them as a medium of conveying ideas addressed to the community. He touched upon such problems as the struggle of young idealists for progress, wasteful emigration, lack of guidance for the peasants, and squandering away national talent. In Sienkiewicz's hands, the short story became an instrument of definite action; its purpose was to stir public opinion and to provoke repercussions. Later, this tendency did not disappear completely, but practical aims were replaced by more general motifs.

In his choice of plots Sienkiewicz was not guided by psychological curiosity or amusement, but by social considerations. Although the incentive arose from anxieties connected with the novelist's own community, his attitude was not parochial. His short stories reflected some of the current problems of his generation, such as the plight of emigrants and the educational issues.

Structurally a number of the stories were ambitious undertakings containing a résumé of the protagonist's life with one striking episode standing out as the main component. Those in this category are "The Lighthouse Keeper of Aspinwall," the portrait of a political refugee; "Lux in Tenebris Lucet," a sketch of an unsuccessful artist; "The Organist from Ponikla," a biography of a country musician; "From the Memoirs of a Poznan Tutor," an account not only of a pupil, but also of a tutor who realized that he was ill with consumption and that his days were numbered. They were not just casual sketches but studied portraits. The intense emotional coloring was tied in with Sienkiewicz's main characters. They were often helpless, born to be victims and provoking compassion.

Sharp contrast was one of the favorite structural devices which the author used in order to enhance the emotional impact of his stories. A satirical attitude was often juxtaposed with that of pathos. Irony was another means which the author introduced with considerable skill.

For a long time, the writer's pessimism weighed heavily on his heroes. Most of the stories ended with the demise of the main characters. The author patiently traced a path of disaster in which human lives were threatened with grief, lunacy, and extinction.

Some incidents kept cropping up in the author's works. In both "Jamiol" and "The Organist from Ponikla," the victims could not walk through deep snow, became tired and sat down, only

to meet their deaths. Another episode the author tended to re-peat was the description of prolonged dying, which occurred in 'Lillian Morris," "Yanko the Musician," "From the Memoirs of a Poznan Tutor," "Lux in Tenebris Lucet," and "Let Us Follow Him." It was fascinating to observe how the identical motifs acquired a different emotional tone.

The effectiveness of some tales depended on their language. In stories dealing with life in the country, the author confronted the peasant dialect with the vulgar jargon of officials and the elaborate elegance of the speech of the gentry. In "Charcoal Sketches" he inserted a parody of typical church sermons, which were so abstract and sublime as to be totally incomprehensible to the parishioners. The *pointe* in "The Lighthouse Keeper of Aspinwall" was dependent upon the poetic charm of *Pan Tadeusz.* "The Tartar Captivity" and "Memories of Mariposa" indicated the writer's fascination with the language of the seventeenth century, which was so important in the *Trilogy*. Among other works the brief "Sabala Fairy Tale" was written in the dialect of the Polish highlanders.

The best stories were probably those in which Sienkiewicz's satirical vein found its expression, e.g., "Bartek the Conqueror", and those with a highly coherent structure and artistic economy, e.g., "The Lighthouse Keeper of Aspinwall."[18]

CHAPTER 4

An Epic Breath

I Search for the Past

THE tale "The Tartar Captivity" (1880) radically differed from the early stories written by Sienkiewicz. Instead of struggling with contemporary evils, he turned to a distant past. Rather than seeking the errors and vices which contributed to the subsequent downfall of the Commonwealth, he filled his narrative with a feeling of admiration and made it a homage to the ancestral chivalrous spirit. No wonder that Positivist critics received the story with anxiety and suspicion. The readers thought otherwise.

The content of the tale is comparable to the poetic drama *El principe constante* (The Constant Prince, 1629) by Calderón, which was wonderfully adapted to the Polish by Slowacki.[1] The hero was a poor member of the gentry named Zdanoborski who fell in love with a senator's daughter. Although the girl reciprocated his feelings, he did not propose to her, as his dignity could not stand any humiliation. He decided that his only chance was to distinguish himself as a soldier, and he joined the armed forces, which were about to depart for the Ukraine. In a battle he was wounded and taken captive by the Tartars. As a prisoner he behaved like a hero. His inflexible attitude challenged common sense. He did not achieve anything, and although he returned to Poland, his life remained miserable. Yet his memoirs sounded like a call to spiritual virtues superior to any practical consideration. They struck a note of pure heroism and honor. The style of the story was also different from his previous tales. It had an authentic quality of the seventeenth century and was comparable in this respect to some of the works of Jozef I. Kraszewski.

The tale signaled a new trend in Sienkiewicz's literary workshop. He began to write his *Trilogy* in 1882. The first part was called *Wolves' Den,* and the author used this title as late as February 1883. At the suggestion of a friend, he changed the title to *With Fire and Sword.* On October 1, 1884 he began work on *The Deluge.* The third novel, *Pan Michael,* was conceived after an interval of a year and a half, in February 1887; it was completed May 5, 1888.

The *Trilogy* occupied more than six years of Sienkiewicz's life. He had to become acquainted with the historical sources, and their study was begun far in advance of the writing of the text. The background of the *Trilogy* embraced over a quarter of a century. *With Fire and Sword* started in the spring of 1647, and the last volume ended with an epilogue describing the Battle of Chocim in 1673. Each novel covered a different war. The first of them centered around the Cossack rebellion (1647–51); *The Deluge* told the story of the military conflict between Poland and Sweden which took place in the middle of the sixth decade; *Pan Michael* started with the election of King Michael Wisniowiecki (1669) and dealt with the clashes of Poland with the Tatars and Turks. The scenes of the novels were laid in various parts of the Commonwealth.

Polish literature of the seventeenth century did not attain the esthetic harmony and poise it had achieved during the Renaissance period. On the other hand, publications and manuscripts were abundant, and quantity partly compensated for lack of quality. The unusual experiences so frequent during periods of war encouraged individuals to record their impressions in memoirs and chronicles in both prose and verse. Documentation referring not only to military events but to daily habits and customs was much richer than in the previous centuries. One of the excellent diarists of the seventeenth century was Jan Pasek, a natural storyteller and a very typical representative of his times.[2]

In the period concerned, contacts with the West were more limited, and cultural isolation was the ineluctable result. Yet it succeeded in creating and developing a specific cultural atmosphere. The Poles produced their own version of the "baroque" style. Its ebullient ornateness and formal richness, sprinkled with Latin quotations, made it a clumsy vehicle for lofty flights of inspiration. Nonetheless, it was picturesque and expressive; and it reflected the ways of life of the period faithfully. One of the positive achievements of the "baroque" trend was a remarkable increase in vocabulary.

Sienkiewicz studied with tireless diligence all the material which could be of value in his formidable task. He perused historical documents, chronicles, monographs, memoirs, and essays; he knew much about all kinds of objects used in the seventeenth century—arms, clothing, furniture, and the like—and he was well acquainted with the literature of the epoch.

Soon after publication of the *Trilogy* was completed Sienkiewicz wrote an essay entitled "On the Historical Novel."[3] It indicated that he was aware of the theoretical dilemma which authors of historical novels were obliged to face. Sienkiewicz quoted the opinion of Georg Brandes that this kind of historical novel was comparable to "genuine fig coffee," which was neither genuine nor coffee. If a novelist said only the truth, argued the Danish critic, he would become a mere historian; if his imagination carried him away, he had to distort the truth, and therefore his work would cease to be historical. Another difficulty resulted from attempts on the part of the writers to identify themselves with people in the past. This was simply not feasible. At best, the historical novels portrayed some external features of bygone life, but this shell encompassed a modern mind. A frequent error lay in attributing major historical developments to minor causes. Dumas, for instance, made his readers believe that some irrelevent romantic affairs were responsible for the wars between England and France.

Sienkiewicz rejected these reservations. He disagreed with the view that historical novelists had to distort the facts. If this actually happened, it arose from the mistakes of the writer, not from the shortcomings of the historical novel as a genre. Should the novel reflect some tendency, it did not differ in this respect from many recognized historical works. After all, even the most prominent historians differed in their judgments of major events and of leading figures. If a novelist included some historical data in his novels, it did not mean his work should be classified as history. Similarly, Sienkiewicz held that elements of physiology in a work of fiction would not qualify it as physiology. History related the most important developments of the past, but it drew only general contours, which were full of gaps. The creative imagination was needed to fill in these gaps. Such an endeavor was comparable to intellectual guessing in scholarly research. Intuition would help in avoiding conflicts with historical truth, which could remain undistorted even though it were rounded out with conjectures, supplements, and comments.

Sienkiewicz believed that it was possible to revive the true spirit animating figures of the past—their thoughts, desires, and passions. There was no truth in the statement that novelists could not represent historical characters. In Sienkiewicz's opinion, the personality of Pasek perpetuated in his memoirs was more accessible and understandable than that of many contemporaries. Inversely, some historical novels made the impression of being authentic documents to such a degree that they might be mistaken for real memoirs.

II *Facts and Opinions*

The essay "On the Historical Novel" presented the author's credo and his own interpretation of the *Trilogy*. It partly justified the objections raised by the critics from the standpoint of history. Controversy on the matter has not yet subsided. Sienkiewicz's critics attacked mainly *With Fire and Sword*, possibly because Polish-Ukrainian relations still remained a burning political issue.

One of the most severe and penetrating judgments came from Boleslaw Prus, a prominent writer and the prospective author of a major historical novel, *The Pharaoh*.[4] In his opinion, Chmielnicki's rebellion was provoked by the powerful Polish magnates whose exploitation and cruelty drove people to despair. Even the Cossacks serving in the Polish armed forces, upon returning to their native land, could not reconcile themselves to the oppression and humiliation to which their people were subjected. The Ukrainian clergy was poor, uneducated, and scorned.

Lawlessness deprived the populace of any personal rights and made it a helpless target of violence and robbery. Gradually the drops of individual hatred swelled into a river of rebellion.

It was true that *With Fire and Sword* did admit the responsibility of the Polish princelings. However, the guilt was also attributed to the Ukrainians. Usually, the Cossacks were shown as a wild, reckless throng, permanently drunk (except during periods of military campaigns), craving blood and booty. In their camp such shocking episodes took place as barbarian murders of their own countrymen, wild lynchings of prisoners and unwanted leaders, and dictatorial maneuvers of wily demagogues. The religious strife which was one of the important aspects of the insurrection was almost ignored.

Samuel Sandler, in his spirited study *Wokol Trylogii* (About the *Trylogy*),[5] showed that in his opinion Sienkiewicz relied mainly on contemporary Polish historians, particularly Kubala and Szajnocha. One might also note that the novelist's version of the Polish-Ukrainian conflict recalled the struggle between the American settlers and the Indians. In the American letters some passages clearly blended Sienkiewicz's impressions of the Wild West with the Ukrainian "Wild Fields":

In the borderland there is no social organization, no towns, no institutions nor laws; there is only a wilderness where an individual, left to himself and to his rifle, does not live a social life. That is why public welfare and social order do not restrain his license and passions. A constant war, constant dangers, assaults, revenges, and the whole wild and raw environment enhance still more individual passions reaching formidable proportions. And it cannot be otherwise. Let us remind ourselves of our borderers settled on the Tatar borders and tracks, and we shall have a similar picture. In spite of the humane disposition prevailing in the old-time community, the borderers were gallant people, fond of war and bloodshed, tempestuous and eager to brawls. Here, in America, the same happens, even in a higher degree . . .[6]

There was a substantial difference between the author's attitude toward individual Cossacks and his treatment of them as a collective body. In *With Fire and Sword* Bohun aroused sometimes more sympathy than his Polish rival Skrzetuski. Bohun's servant Zakhar was certainly less objectionable than Rzedzian.

Various passages of the *Trilogy* pointed out that the Cossacks were fine soldiers. Yet the Ukrainian Army as a whole gave the impression of a mob, incalculable and undisciplined, guided by sinister instincts rather than by the orders of their officers, and winning some battles due to sheer numerical superiority.

In the 1930's a historian, Olgierd Gorka, subjected *With Fire and Sword* to a detailed scrutiny.[7] He paid special attention to Jeremiah Wisniowiecki, the most controversial figure in the novel. Sienkiewicz made him a brilliant commander, a patriotic citizen, and a providential statesman who succeeded in staving off the perils threatening the Commonwealth. Gorka represented Jeremiah as a coward who fled several times from the battlefields and increased his wealth by plunder. In his opinion, Jeremiah was master of self-advertising, and his real aim was to acquire independent political and military power on the eastern bank of the Dnieper. Chmielnicki had reason to be grateful to him, as Jeremiah abstained from supporting other Polish commanders in the early stages of the rising.[8]

The verdict of Gorka met with vigorous opposition. W. Tomkiewicz asserted that after the initial defeats suffered by the Poles no compromise was possible with the rebels and a display of military power was the only means to restore peace. Wisniowiecki realized this and became the main exponent of what he considered the only sensible policy. His supposed cowardice was reasonable behavior based on sound military considerations. The portrait painted by Sienkiewicz closely resembled the real Jeremiah, showing not only good qualities but also shortcomings and even vices.[9]

These heated discussions showed that the political aspect of *With Fire and Sword* overshadowed its other aspects. In America J. Curtin preceded his translation of the novel with a preface written in a pro-Russian mood. He described the Russians as liberators of the Ukraine and guardians of Orthodoxy. To counterbalance the effect of the epilogue, which told of the Polish victory at Beresteczko, Curtin gave a detailed description of the subsequent defeat of the Poles at Batog. Moreover, he appended to *The Deluge*, where almost nothing was told about Ukraine, a passage reporting the submission of Chmielnicki and his army to the Russian tsar. The translator not only ignored the Ukrainian pursuit of national independence, but the very existence of the Ukrainians as a separate nation, provoking a protest of the Polish novelist.[10]

A degree of bias was also manifested in other parts of the *Trilogy*. For the sake of illustration, one could observe that no political motifs of the Swedish invasion were cited, making it appear as if pillage was the exclusive reason for the Polish-Swedish War. However, in view of the defensive attitude of the Poles, *The Deluge* created the impression of being a more objective work.

The prolonged and passionate discussion of the political bias in the *Trilogy* contributed little to the understanding of its literary worth. Sometimes the critics overlooked the fact that, in his approach to the historical material, the writer did not differ from other authors who felt authorized to render an individual interpretation of history. In his poem *Poltava* Alexander Pushkin presented the Ukrainian patriotic rebel Mazeppa as a Russian traitor and attached to him the epithet *zlodei* (villain). Likewise, the image of Napoleon in *War and Peace* by Tolstoy gave the impression of a satirical sally.

The concentration of the novelist on the seventeenth century was a result of careful reflection. In his review of Ludwik Kubala's historical essays the novelist spoke of the decaying organism of the Commonwealth, unable to withstand the impending storms.[11] Nonetheless, in the *Trilogy* he turned to the past, not in order to spread doubts and despair, but "to comfort the hearts." This aim he admitted clearly and emphatically in the postscript to *Pan Michael*. Severe condemnation of seventeenth-century Poland made such task awkward. Any other era of national history might have been more suitable for the author's objective.

How did Sienkiewicz solve this predicament? He did not attempt to whitewash the faults and fallacies of the Commonwealth. He stressed its historical and cultural role, but he also pointed to many humiliating episodes, such as Pilawce, where a mightly Polish Army panicked before the Cossack offensive, and the occupation of the Polish territory, including the capital, by the Swedish forces. However, he manipulated the lights and shadows in such a way that the cumulative effect was plausible. Sometimes it was not necessary to misinterpret historical events; it was sufficient to describe the Polish victories in a more detailed way and to report the defeats indirectly by one of the eyewitnesses.[12] The order of incidents was also important. Every novel showed that after painful tests, the respective campaigns ended with a final triumph of Poland. This was natural in *The Deluge* and *Pan Michael,* as both the Swedes and Turks met defeats. In *With Fire and Sword,* the epilogue told of a major Cossack disaster at Beresteczko, although this was not the end of the war.

Notwithstanding the failures of the Commonwealth, the writer contended that it continued to play a constructive function. In *With Fire and Sword,* he attributed to it the expansion of civilization in the East. In *The Deluge,* he demonstrated the role of Catholicism. *Pan Michael* showed Sobieski, the future Polish king, not merely as the defender of his own country, but also of Christendom.

Among the characters introduced in the *Trilogy,* there were traitors, wranglers, rakes, scoundrels, and ordinary criminals. Yet the main heroes, although not necessarily people of high caliber, were decent, respectable citizens. They might have displayed various human weaknesses and even committed grave mistakes, but they maintained a certain amount of decency which safeguarded them from baseness. Among them, Skrzetuski was a conspicuous exception, appearing too faultless and monumental.

Sienkiewicz believed in the spiritual health of his countrymen. This faith inspired the incidents in *The Deluge.* Kmicic was condemned not only by his friends and neighbors, but by his beloved girl as well. He had committed so many abuses that the law considered him a criminal deserving capital punishment. He also joined the camp of traitors and rendered them important services. However, his deeds resulted from genuine convictions. As soon as he learned the truth, he changed drastically and redeemed all his sins. His behavior was to illustrate the unshakable firmness of moral values based on patriotism and religion.

The *Trilogy* resounded like a hymn of vigor and vitality. The instances of physical prowess and dexterity emerged not as isolated cases but as typical manifestations of the soundness and strength of the whole community. This emphasis on physical values[13] coincided with a more general trend, which produced the restoration of the Olympic Games in 1896 and concurred with the most universal of Sienkiewicz's novels, *Quo Vadis?*.

The optimistic lesson which the author succeeded in extracting from his excursion into the national past was badly needed by his countrymen. The failure of armed resistance in 1863 and the subsequent reprisals produced a mood of depression. Moderate successes achieved in the social and industrial field were disappointing. Small wonder that people sought relief in history; but the historians did not satisfy their need. The Cracow group exalted the past errors as the only causes of Poland's downfall. This unilateral criticism met with strong opposition. Even the poet Adam Asnyk, a "Red" during the January Uprising, protested against the verdicts of the "new historical school."[14] The balm of faith offered by the novelist was received with gratitude and relief.

III *Marks of Life*

The texture of the *Trilogy* belonged to history, but some recent incidents also left their mark. During the long work on the cycle many events occurred to which the writer could not remain indifferent. When he started to write *With Fire and Sword*, there were reports of anti-Semitic disturbances taking place in some Ukrainian cities. These might have inspired the wild mob scenes included in the novel.

In his short stories Sienkiewicz admitted that he did not value the peasants as a reliable political power. It was not surprising that in the first part of the *Trilogy* he resorted mainly to portrayal of the gentry and magnates. Such a biased depiction of the community met with sharp criticism, which in turn compelled the writer to revise his judgment. In *The Deluge* many magnates (e.g., the Radziwills, Radziejowski, Opalinski, and others) were presented as traitors conspiring with the enemies during the peril of the Commonwealth. Czarniecki, the main leader of the military campaign against the Swedes, was quite different than the wealthy princeling Jeremiah Wisniowiecki in *With Fire and Sword*. Czarniecki was not a magnate but a relatively obscure officer who liked to say of himself that he had grown not from the fields or from the salt mines but from his pain, that is, that he did not owe his career to the sale of grain or salt but to his military service and to the blood shed on the battlefields.[15]

Logically enough, the active role of different social classes in the liberation of the country was now emphatically stressed. The first military and moral successes in the struggle against the Swedish invaders were due not to any single military leader but to the general upsurge following the successful defense of the national shrine at Czestochowa. After this, the defeat of the invaders became only a matter of time. The man who occasioned the sudden turn of events was a monk and the prior of a monastery; he resisted all threats and temptations and inspired the little garrison of the fortress.

In *The Deluge* the burghers not only cooperated in the defense of the monastery but displayed outstanding courage; some of them, including a local beggar woman, were real heroes. Townsmen were involved in many other military events. Peasants likewise did not remain inactive; they struck against the enemy at every opportunity. A most significant episode occurred in the Tatra Mountains. When King Jan Kazimierz returned from exile, he found himself facing a new danger. Upon encountering a large unit of Swedish soldiers, he came close to falling prisoner in their hands despite the gallantry of his retinue. At a crucial moment, the local highlanders intervened; they ambushed the Swedes and defeated them completely. The King was so impressed that he promised to introduce a law improving the social standing of the peasants.[16]

On another occasion a simple teen-aged peasant lad, Michalko, relayed the news to a Polish unit that the Swedish king was staying with a small group of soldiers in a neighboring parsonage. The commander asked Michalko what reward he would like for this information. He simply requested a saber in order to fight in the battle. During the skirmish, the boy behaved gallantly, even capturing an enemy banner. He hardly noticed that he was wounded. Czarniecki was amazed at this and promised to confer on him gentry rank at the first meeting of the Polish Sejm.[17]

If the peasant fighters made some mistakes, it was due to a lack of experience, not to lack of gallantry. Kmicic learned from his subordinates that the highlanders, armed with hatchets, tried to occupy Cracow. Since they had no experience in fighting in the plains, General Douglas easily dispersed them; but not a single man returned from the Swedish units sent after them into the mountains.[18] Whenever the officers organized armed detachments, the peasants and servants joined them.

From the first day of the siege of Czestochowa, the peace-loving and patient plowmen seized their scythes and assisted the gentry in their struggle. The more farsighted Swedish generals looked with the greatest anxiety at these growing clouds, which could cause a deluge. They tried to terrorize the peasants by repression. They severed their right hands and mercilessly executed them; but the spirit of the plowmen was undaunted. Over thirty similar references to their bravery can be found in different chapters of *The Deluge*. Some villages were practically deserted because all male inhabitants joined in the fight.

Among the peasants were specimens of unusual physical strength. In the spectacle organized by Lubomirski, a highlander, a kind of peasant Samson, threw a millstone up and caught it in mid-air. The common people were invited to a reception for soldiers.[19] The king summoned the entire populace to war. It was their chance to acquire honors, prerogatives, and benefits possessed by the gentry.[20] A great number of villages between the San and Vistula rivers belonged to the Marshal and his relatives. All the peasants residing in this area rebelled against the foe, as the Marshal, sparing no fortune, promised to emancipate all those who took up arms.[21] Finally, the king made the pledge that he would take care of the poor community of plowmen. The clergy, senators, gentry, and all the people listened to this solemn declaration delivered in the cathedral in Lwow in the presence of the Papal nuncio.[22] Sienkiewicz did not make any man of lower social standing a leading actor in the plot, but left no doubt that he attributed the liberation of the country to all social strata.

This democratic trend continued in *Pan Michael*. There the protagonist was the most modest of the leading figures in the *Trilogy*. Although he had served in the army for many years, he received no reward and remained poor. Sobieski, in a frank conversation, told him that even if people ignored his merits, he should just clench his teeth and repeat the words, "For thee, my country." The hetman dreamed of a fraternity of such devoted soldiers as the most reliable mainstay of the motherland.[23] This idea was directly opposed to the prior confidence placed in such leaders as Wisniowiecki.

Sienkiewicz's preoccupation with the Prussian danger found a curious reflection in *The Deluge*. The writer singled out the magnates of the western province, Opalinski and Radziejowski, as the first traitors surrendering to the Swedes. During his visit to Poznan, he obtained firsthand information of the local political problems.[24] The treacherous action on the part of the western magnates in the seventeenth century sounded like a hint of contemporary dangers. It was significant that Radziejowski and Opalinski introduced by the novelist in the first volume never reappeared in the novel and were quite unnecessary from the standpoint of its structure.[25] Further, Prussia looked in *The Deluge* as a minor military power, which fell easy victim of the Polish forces; and its formal dependence on Poland was often mentioned.

The author's treatment of the Russians was more discreet. Although Muscovy took a very active part in the Cossack and Swedish wars, its name could not appear in the *Trilogy* because of censorship. If the writer had to introduce the Muscovites, he usually referred to them as the *Septentriones* (the Northerners).

Some allusions to the contemporary relations between the Poles and their partitioners, although well-disguised, were obvious to the readers attuned to such cryptic messages. The situation of the invaded Commonwealth in *The Deluge* afforded them a comparison with the partitioned Poland. Zagloba, whom Sienkiewicz often used as his mouthpiece, once met his friends immediately after the news of a major defeat. The swashbuckler predicted new battles which might be won or lost but which would not alter the final outcome of the war:

Listen, as you will not hear this from an ordinary mouth, because not everyone can review things in a general way. What is still in store for us? How many battles? How many defeats must one expect in a war against such a commander as King Charles . . . how many tears, how much blood will be shed? And some people begin to doubt and offend the grace of God and His Mother . . . But I say to you: do you know what will be the lot of those vandals? Peril! Do you know what will happen to us? Victory! They may still beat us a hundred times . . . well, but we shall win the hundredth and first battle and this will be the end of it.—Here Zagloba closed his eyes for a moment and suddenly shouted with the whole might of his lungs:—Victory!—[26]

Naturally, the author's countrymen interpreted this statement as a watchword applicable to the future. The same appeal sounded in the speech of Zagloba during the wedding of Kmicic:

Gentlemen! to the honor of future generations. God bless them and allow them to safeguard the heritage regained by our work, sweat, and blood which we bequeath to them . . . and when difficult times come, let them think of us and never despair, considering that there are no such predicaments from which we would not be able to recover *viribus unitis* and with God's help.[27]

Such links with then current problems enriched the texture of the *Trilogy* and added to its emotional vigor. It could be taken by the readers not only as a historical narrative but as a camouflaged struggle with timely, burning issues as well. This made the *Trilogy* more meaningful to Sienkiewicz's countrymen; but its initial success among foreign admirers resulted only from its narrative value and qualities of craftsmanship.

IV *The Epic Craft*

The historical novel as a literary genre was well established and had a respectable tradition in Polish literature. The disillusionment with current events produced a turn to the past. This attitude coincided with a general trend during the Romantic period. The most influential model for European writers was Sir Walter Scott, whose stories of adventure, suspense, and customs set against a historical backdrop won him international popularity.[28] As early as the beginning of the nineteenth century, Julian Ursyn Niemcewicz adopted some of the devices of the Scottish master. Bernatowicz, Czajkowski, Krasinski, Rzewuski, Kraszewski, and others were Sienkiewicz's predecessors. Among them, Jozef I. Kraszewski conceived and realized the idea of presenting the entire history of Poland in a series of novels. Kraszewski was one of the fine connoisseurs of the seventeenth century, and he devoted twelve of his narratives to this period. Sienkiewicz was also familiar with Russian fiction based on the history of the Ukraine: *Taras Bulba* by Gogol and *The Captain's Daughter* by Pushkin.

The mixture of history and adventure was popularized by Alexandre Dumas. Some superficial resemblances between the French writer and Sienkiewicz were evident. Both authors took a liking to the seventeenth century; both devised a cycle of novels embracing a few decades with considerable gaps of time among separate links.[29] The two writers maintained the continuity of the whole cycle by invariably preserving a number of characters. Both devoted an important part of their novels to chivalrous feats, military incidents, and ingenious stratagems.

The differences were even more striking. For Dumas the historical background was a mere pretext for adventures; important events were presented in a sketchy, blurred, inconclusive manner. It would be frustrating to turn to his novels as a source of historical information. Sienkiewicz treated the past with much more respect. In *The Three Musketeers* and its sequel, the chain of incidents was artificial and elaborate. For the Polish novelist, the adventurous element was one of the organic ingredients of warfare, and he treated it as an attribute of the era. He knew that adventures were a dominant component in Pasek's authentic memoirs and that they reflected faithfully some aspects of the period; he mirrored them in the *Trilogy*.[30] In this respect, he was closer to Victor Hugo and Emile Zola.

A more solid historical background, its wide scope, and national coloring raised the *Trilogy* to epic proportions. This was the view of some early critics who introduced Sienkiewicz to the English-speaking world. Military episodes prevailed in a decisive way, but a number of scenes referred to various aspects of ordinary life: crafts, trades, entertainments, political activities, religious ceremonies, and so forth. Individual actions and mass scenes presented the community as a coherent, collective body.

The epic design was enhanced by some typically Homeric devices. As in the *Iliad*, some battle scenes included duels in which individual heroes gained prominence, e.g., Longinus, Pan Michael, Kmicic, Bohun, and even the ubiquitous Zagloba. Sienkiewicz indulged in hyperbolic descriptions, as in the case of Longinus, who acquired superhuman stature. The similes confronting the world of men with nature, inserted mainly in battle episodes, marked the elemental complexion of human warfare. One of the distinctive similes appeared in the final part of *The Deluge*:

. . . as when a lordly lion, pierced the moment before with missiles, rises suddenly, and shaking his kingly mane, roars mightily, pale terror pierces straightway the hunters, and their feet turn to flight; so that Commonwealth rose ever more terrible, filled with the anger of Jove, ready to meet the whole world. Into the bones of the aggressors there entered weakness and fear; not of plunder were they thinking then, but of this only, to bear away home sound heads from the jaws of the lion.[31]

The analogies between the *Trilogy* and the Homeric epic occurred to many American critics. The most detailed parallel between the *Iliad* and the *Trilogy* was developed in an anonymous introduction to *Without Dogma* (1893):

His warriors fight, love, hate; they embrace each other; they laugh; they weep in each other's arms; give each other sage counsels, with a truly Homeric simplicity. They are deep-versed in stratagems of love and war, these Poles of the seventeenth century! They have their Nestor, their Agamemnon, their Achilles sulking in his tent. Oddly enough, at times they grow very familiar to us, and in spite of their Polish titles and faces, and a certain tenderness of nature that is almost feminine, they seem to have good, stout Saxon stuff in them.[32]

Recently Szweykowski produced a different theory, suggesting that Sienkiewicz intended to write a legend of the national past rather than a truly epic work.[33] If this interpretation were to be accepted, it would scamp the writer's careful and systematic study of historical sources and his defense of the historical novel as a legitimate literary genre. Moreover, his contemporaries received the *Trilogy* as a truly historical narrative, and it would hardly be reasonable to assume that the author's estimate of his own book differed so drastically from that of his readers. For succeeding generations of Poles, the historical material contained in the work became less significant and was overshadowed by the fictional components. Naturally enough, they began to attribute to the work a legendary flavoring. However, this was due rather to the changed attitude of the readers than to the intricate qualities of the *Trilogy*.[34]

The traditional devices of the mystery novels influenced the *Trilogy* in but a few minor details. No secrets survive in it for extensive periods of time. No mysterious figures with enigmatic pasts are involved; the earthly descent of every person is clearly defined; and riddles (as in the case of Zagloba) are treated in a humorous way. But the *Trilogy* abounds in occurrences typical of the novel of adventure: rivalry for the love of one woman, kidnappings, escapes, pursuits, apparent perils, miraculous rescues, partings of lovers for lengthy periods of time and their final reunions, masquerades under assumed names, and so on. Closely interrelated are descriptions of reckless courage as well as of ingenious tricks produced in desperate situations.

Sienkiewicz did not hesitate to submit the credulity of his readers to trying tests. Kmicic was in mortal danger so many times that his survival was little short of a miracle. Even more surprising were the experiences of the women. Helena in *With Fire and Sword,* Olenka in *The Deluge,* Basia in *Pan Michael,* all fell into the hands of men passionately in love with them. Although they were practically defenseless, they succeeded in remaining untarnished and in regaining their freedom.[35] Naturally, it would be wrong to apply to these incidents the normal criteria of probability, — they belonged to an accepted literary convention. Moreover, the tempo of action was so swift and the author's story so enthralling that many overstrained situations escaped critical vigilance.

A historian could admit that the periods of prolonged wars usually produced adventurers thriving in the surrounding chaos and specializing in the exploitation of their luck. This was characteristic of the seventeenth century when professional soldiers flourished. They served in different armies and considered warfare as their chance of making a career and accumulating wealth. Kmicic was such a knight of fortune: he knew perfectly well how to enrich himself and his subordinates, even if he fought in his own country. It should be added that the author's vision of the Commonwealth's southeastern territory, with its unsettled conditions, provided the ideal background for guerrilla warfare. This coordination between the adopted technique, the era, and the territory elevated the *Trilogy* above the usual level of the novel of adventure.

The number of people delineated by Sienkiewicz in the work is certainly impressive. Although the gentry prevail, other social classes are also represented. Attention is focused on the professional and volunteer soldiers of all possible ranks and detachments. A number of characters are of foreign extraction—Cossacks, Germans, Tatars, Swedes, Czechs, and even a Scotsman (Ketling). As if the author intended to confirm the Latin saying, *Inter arma silent Musae,* no intellectuals appear in active roles. Schools and academies are virtually invisible. As to the theater, it finds an indirect reference in a tale of Pan Michael in the early part of *The Deluge.* Preparations for the election of the new kings provide the backdrop of political life. The clergymen are allowed to preach on a few occasions; yet Prior Kordecki, the defender of Czestochowa, is a fighter rather than an eloquent preacher.

The writer presented his characters in a two-dimensional way. His portraits lacked the effect of inner depth. Their psychological problems were relatively simple. The scale of their spiritual experiences was predetermined and their behavior predictable. Most of them conformed with their epoch, and the author usually succeeded in making them believable and easily distinguishable. The early Polish readers treated them like really existing persons: they enjoyed their successes, deplored their failures and misfortunes, prayed for their salvation and even ordered masses after their death. The reaction of the foreign readers was cooler, but mostly flattering for the novelist.

Sienkiewicz draws his human portraits with sharp, distinct lines. The behavior of his characters often oscillates between contrasting moral extremes: patriotism and treason, self-sacrifice and egoism, piety and heresy, discipline and anarchy, duty and lawlessness. Only a few figures are presented in a derogatory way, such as both Radziwills and a group of magnates in western Poland. Kuklinowski in *The Deluge* appears as a villain, repulsive and without a conscience. Some of these wicked individuals are accorded punishment. Janusz Radziwill was defeated and died; Kuklinowski was subjected to the same cruel torture he started to inflict on Kmicic. On the other hand, Boguslaw Radziwill, a cynical traitor, not only survived all trials but in *Pan Michael* reappeared as a potential candidate to the Polish throne; and his henchman Sakowicz made a successful career.[36]

Clearly defined moral criteria, eliminating doubt and sophistry, were desirable for a people divided and subjected to the pressures and temptations of contradictory allegiances. In view of possible confusion, distinct principles had some didactic advantages. On the other hand, such simplification resulted in a superficial treatment of more intricate psychological problems.

During the long years of toiling over the *Trilogy*, the novelist became attached to his own creations to such a degree that he regarded them almost as personal acquaintances. If he disliked any of them, he quickly removed them from the stage, as happened with Kuklinowski. As for those he liked, he permitted them certain privileges. He gave them a chance to recover from defeat, bestowed upon them successes and honors, and allowed them to get rid of their faults and gain the favor of his readers. In such a way Kmicic earned a moral promotion.

Zagloba became not only a great favorite of the public but of his creator as well. He resembled the ancient humorous characters ironically called *miles gloriosus*. He was sometimes compared to Falstaff, but the analogies with his Shakespearian predecessor were misleading. Zagloba was above all a natural product of his native background. He was partly based on Rudolf Korwin

Piotrowski, one of the novelist's Polish-American acquaintances. Zagloba owed to this picturesque individual his most striking features: jovial wit, inexhaustible ingenuity, fondness for fantastic lies, weakness for the fair sex notwithstanding his advanced age, and insatiable thirst. A caricature drawn by Sienkiewicz demonstrated that Zagloba's outlook was also modeled on Piotrowski's. Modjeska described this gentleman as a typical seventeenth-century figure who miraculously survived to modern times, preserving vitality, humor, and specific diction.[37] Yet, it would be erroneous to consider Zagloba as the picture of any single individual. Some of the writer's friends noticed a resemblance between the "Polish Ulysses" and Sienkiewicz's father-in-law. The novelist once told Curtin that similar characters were not uncommon among the Poles and that he knew two persons in Warsaw who reminded him strongly of Zagloba.

At first Zagloba appeared to be a nondescript sycophant, not particular about his company, and ready to drink with anyone who would pay for his liquor. Even his patriotic loyalty aroused some doubts. However, in crucial moments, he followed his conscience and his sense of honor. He did not like to risk his neck unnecessarily, but in real need he displayed courage and, when furious, he fought like a hero. He enjoyed boasting of his fantastic deeds. As a friend, he was invaluable; but, at times, he embarrassed his companions when he asked them to confirm events which had never taken place.

For a long time Zagloba remained more amusing than respectable. Eventually the funny gentleman acquired more dignity. He became commander of a large military camp. In *Pan Michael* he received a visit from the vice-chancellor and, although slightly embarrassed by this unexpected honor, he conducted the conversation with such skill that his prestige increased.

The author treated his Ulysses with warm sentiment mixed with mischief. He made him an exponent of his sense of humor and the target of his practical jokes. Sienkiewicz enjoyed putting him in awkward situations and letting him extricate himself from these traps. During the siege of Warsaw in *The Deluge*, the writer involved him in a heroic battle with monkeys. Usually Zagloba appeared as a clever, experienced man whose advice was most valuable and who understood human nature. However, when already a respected man, he committed a blunder which almost caused a tragedy. Zagloba planned a marriage between Pan Michael and Basia, but the colonel preferred Krystyna. In order to bring his plan to fruition, Zagloba encouraged a romance between Krystyna and Ketling. As a result, a duel between the two rivals seemed inevitable. Zagloba was worried and felt responsible for this confusion. He sought Wolodyjowski in vain and returned desperate, only to discover that everything turned out well despite his clumsy meddling. The great sage who solved so many riddles failed completely in this criss-cross Marivaudage.[38]

Zagloba's vital role was preserved throughout the *Trilogy*, except toward the end of the work when he was an octogenarian and became less active. Structurally, he seemed to interfere with other elements in the *Trilogy* and with its dominating mood, but without his appearances, the atmosphere would be too gloomy. He struck a note of cheerfulness whenever hopelessness became too oppressive. Yet he was not a conventional figure comparable to comical characters in the Italian *Commedia del arte* and the farces. Zagloba brought to the fore an important aspect of seventeenth-century Poland. Humor was one of its staple ingredients. People not only sought all kinds of jokes, puns, anecdotes, witticisms, funny nicknames, and proverbs, but valued them and preserved them for posterity in individual collections of curiosities and memorable incidents called *Silvae rerum*. This tendency found reflection in literature. Many outstanding poets, including Rey, Kochanowski, Szarzynski, Potocki, and Kochowski, wrote "trifles," brief jocular poems, original or translated from other languages. Zagloba reflected this widespread fancy. Sometimes his antics would seem vulgar, but such was the taste of his epoch.

V *The Master's Workshop*

Physical traits of the characters were drawn with confident precision. They included not just a general description of postures and faces, but gaits, gestures, temper, and so on. The writer was always aware of their reaction to varying conditions. The coarse conduct of Kmicic's companions changed completely during their visit to Olenka's home. Longinus, a formidable giant, was the kindest and most inoffensive person in everyday contacts, but on the battlefield he spread fear and horror. Thus Sienkiewicz's heroes behaved not as puppets obeying the master's strings but as autonomous human beings. In view of the great number of actors, it was essential to combine them in such a way that their individual traits would acquire a more distinctive look. This could be noted in connection with a group of the main characters who were made cordial friends, namely Zagloba, Skrzetuski, Longinus, and Pan Michael. Longinus was a lean giant, Wolodyjowski a man of small stature, Skrzetuski an imposing knightly figure, and Zagloba a stout man advancing in age. Together they made a team as memorable as Dumas' three musketeers with their brilliant recruit, D'Artagnan. Another device used by Sienkiewicz was to concentrate on a limited number of selected characters. There were large portions of the text in which some of the major actors disappeared temporarily to allow the readers to get better acquainted with other figures.

Feminine portraits in the *Trilogy* are less significant. They lack a definite connection with their era and seem to be products of the author's abstract images. Olenka Billewicz appears as a strong character and a paragon of patriotism, but her unwavering, monumental dignity is psychologically unconvincing. Other romantic heroines are conventional beauties lacking personality. Anusia and Basia seem natural enough, but their behavior is automatic and their reactions are repetitive. Despite their childlike charm, their appeal is limited. A more intriguing feminine type is Princess Kurcewicz, a forceful character ruling her family with iron discipline; but she comes on the scene early and is soon withdrawn from the narrative. The female characters mainly serve a structural function as participants in romantic episodes.

Diction contributed to the distinctness of individuals. In a few cases, Sienkiewicz supplied his characters with specific sayings (Longinus) or with sharply accentuated dialectical idioms. He carefully coordinated the style used by different persons with their mental and emotional characteristics. Both Zagloba and

Pan Michael are witty, but the old man is usually good humored, while the wit of the latter becomes a sharp weapon, almost as deadly as his sword.

The structure of the *Trilogy* is better appreciated when it is remembered that each novel appeared initially in periodical installments. In this regard, the Polish writer followed the example set by English and French writers. Charles Dickens published *The Pickwick Papers* in twenty monthly portions, of which the first was printed in April 1836 and the last in November 1837, with but one interval in June 1837.[39] In France Emile de Girardin conceived a similar idea; on August 5, 1836 *Le Siècle* began to reprint chapters of a famous Spanish tale *Lazarillo de Tormes*. A couple of months later *La Presse* started to print Balzac's novel *La vieille fille* from the series *Scènes de la vie de province*, which appeared in twelve installments. After 1840, almost all prominent French writers serialized their novels in the daily press prior to their issue as separate books. In like manner, Alfred de Musset published some of his *Comédies et proverbes*.[40] The fashion spread to other countries, including Russia. Some drawbacks of serialization were noticed by French critics who found it perilous to literary craftsmanship and protested against its abuses. One of the most obvious difficulties was the writer's inability to see the work as a whole and to add the necessary final touches.

In Poland serialization was not only a vogue and a means of increasing the author's income, but a necessity. The books had to be passed by the censors of the three respective states; such procedure was an embarrassing and risky affair. The risk could be reduced if the work came out gradually in small installments. Moreover, a substantial increase of the author's fees meant more in Poland than in the wealthier Western countries. Finally, the author gained an opportunity of following more closely the reaction of his readership residing in different occupied sections of Poland.

In a conversation with Curtin, Sienkiewicz described his own method of serializing his novels.[41] At first he devised a detailed plan, which he carefully wrote down. He memorized the plan and let it "seethe and ferment." When he felt prepared to write, he divided the available time not into days but into weeks. During the first week, he produced a certain amount of text and continued this procedure week after week. If the novel was printed in a daily, the editors could divide each installment into daily portions. The author did not rigidly follow his initial plan, but allowed for various changes produced by "seething and fermentation." Presumably, he had little reserve material.

The printing of the first novel of the *Trilogy* in serialized form was treated as an experiment. It appeared simultaneously in the daily *Slowo* (Warsaw) from May 2, 1883 until March 1, 1884; and in *Czas* (Cracow) from May 3, 1883 to March 5, 1884. The test proved successful, and it was only slightly modified when *The Deluge* was made available. It appeared in Warsaw (*Slowo*, Dec. 23, 1884, to Sept. 10, 1886); Cracow (*Czas*, Dec. 24, 1884, to Sept. 2, 1886); and Poznan (*Dziennik Poznanski*, Dec. 25, 1884, to Sept. 7, 1886). Altogether, publication took over twenty months. The same three dailies began to print *Pan Michael* on June 2, 1887 and continued its serialization until the middle of May 1888.

As might be expected, the serial publication created trouble. When *With Fire and Sword* began to appear, only part of the text was ready, and Sienkiewicz feared that the printing would catch up with him and would compel him to write new installments from day to day.[42] The other concern was with the necessity of maintaining cohesion and continuity in the novels. The author relied on the thorough groundwork of which he spoke to Curtin. He also acquired the habit of working systematically, maintaining fixed hours wherever he happened to be. In view of the length of the novels, even these precautionary measures would not have sufficed were it not for his excellent memory. Last but not least, he elaborated some structural means which helped to safeguard continuity.[43]

From the very start, Sienkiewicz introduced in *With Fire and Sword* a device aimed at maintaining cohesion in the story. He anticipated prospective events by referring to the widespread custom of predicting the future by observing nature:

The year 1647 was that wonderful year in which manifold signs in the heavens and on the earth announced misfortunes of some kind and unusual events . . . (Myriads of locusts swarmed from the wilderness

[98]

in early springtime, which was a sign of the imminent Tartar invasion) . In the summer there was a great eclipse of the sun, and soon after a comet appeared in the sky . . . Since such an order of things appeared altogether unnatural, all men . . . who were waiting or looking for unusual events turned their excited minds and eyes especially to the wilderness, from which rather than anywhere else danger might show itself.[44]

This augury referred to the general sequence of incidents which were to be related in the novel. It reappeared once again when Skrzetuski rescued an unknown gentleman who introduced himself at first as Habdank and later revealed his real name, Chmielnicki: "The day of judgment is already on the road through the wilderness, and when it comes all God's world would be amazed."[45] Here the forecast was somewhat more concrete than in the initial passage.

Another gloomy foreboding came from Vassily, the eldest of the Kurcewicz brothers, blinded by the infidels, who greeted the guests with the words: "Woe to you, brothers, woe to me, since we made war for booty: . . . for us the hour of liberation has not come. Woe to you, brothers! Woe to me!"[47] In another chapter Zagloba announced: ". . . difficult times are coming for the gentry: *dies irae et calamitatis.*"[48] Such forecasts prepared the mood and created an expectation. Some of them reflected pre-judices and beliefs of the people, tinging the narrative with local color.

At first there was no hint of a romantic affair. However, when Skrzetuski met the two young ladies whose journey was inter-rupted by the breaking down of their carriage, a strange thing happened: ". . . suddenly a wonderful omen was seen. The falcon, leaving one foot on the hand of the lady, caught with the other foot the hand of the lieutenant, and instead of going to it began to scream joyfully and put the hands together with such power that they touched."[46] The development of the romance was quite complicated, and many episodes contradicted the omen, but it could not be erased. The same prediction was repeated in a jocular form, when Helena asked the cuckoo how long she would live with the Lieutenant, and he wanted to know how many boys they would have.

The forecasts were even more frequent in the longest novel of the *Trilogy*, *The Deluge*. Once more people observed sinister signs in nature: "A superstitious fear seized the human hearts. Many said that these wars so unfortunate and these unheard of calamities were attached to the royal name. People explained willingly that the letters on the coins meant not only *Ioannes Casimirus Rex* but also *Initium Calamitatis Regni* (Beginning of the disaster of the Kingdom).[49] Other strange new phenomena would be observed in spring.

A different kind of premonition preceded the peril awaiting the companions of Kmicic. When they were expelled from Olenka's manor they were furious. As soon as they bypassed the first trees of the forest, a huge flock of crows whirled above their heads. Zend croaked shrilly, and thousands of voices answered him from above. The flock came down so low that the horses were frightened by the rustle of their wings. One of the comrades told Zend to shut up, but others only laughed. The crows flew lower and lower, so that the party rode as if through a storm. "Fools! they could not guess the bad omen!" interjected the author. Indeed, in a brawl the adventurers were killed.[50] Here the forecast referred to the next event and had no major structural purpose.

A purely structural foreboding was inserted in the third volume.[51] Kmicic already renounced his mistakes, abandoned the Radziwills, and decided to repent; but as to his romantic affair, it reached a standstill. He rescued an elderly gentleman besieged by German and Swedish rogues and was received in the man's home. The host believed that the day of wrath would come, but his daughter recalled the prophecy of Saint Brigit which foretold the defeat of the enemies, inflicted by someone who would not spare his soul for love of truth. There were so many obvious coincidences that Kmicic naturally interpreted them as a favorable presage of his own future. This scene preceded a long line of incidents which separated the lovers and exposed them to dangers. The remembrance of the benign augury safeguarded the optimistic hope for the future and kept the romance alive.

Another means of strengthening the unity was the use of flashbacks. They were especially helpful when they were repetitive and showed the same episode from different angles. Sometimes such retrospective glances referred to single episodes. In *The Deluge*, the successful blowing up of the greatest Swedish gun by Kmicic filled a considerable part of the seventeenth and eighteenth chapters of the third volume. Captured by the Swedes, Kmicic related frankly how he performed this assignment.[52] When the siege of Czestochowa was almost over, Prior Kordecki and his officers disclosed his real name and exalted his last exploit. In the meantime, Kmicic joined the retinue of the King and, reporting the events at Czestochowa, he had to retell the episode. Once again the incident reappeared when Kmicic, accompanied by Zagloba and Pan Michael, was admitted to the Swedish king. Finally, King Kazimierz mentioned the event in his message restoring Kmicic's good name. A desperate attempt of Kmicic to kidnap Boguslaw Radziwill was reported by the magnate to his brother (7, III); Kmicic repeated the story to the king (7, IV), and later to Pan Michael (13, IV); Sapieha mentioned it to his officers (17, IV).

Sometimes the author recapitulated not only outstanding exploits but also the larger portions of incidents. Boguslaw Radziwill's long courtship of Olenka is at first told briefly by an eyewitness, Ketling, but afterward Sienkiewicz devotes three chapters to the same theme. The initial offenses of Kmicic with which the reader is already well acquainted are the subject of his confession to Olenka.[53] Kmicic repeats some sordid details of his biography to Pan Michael,[54] and a little later he reports them to Janusz Radziwill before resuming his military duties.[55] He tells many facts from his life to the King (7, IV), at first concealing certain details which could not be prematurely revealed. On various occasions he recalls his former experiences to his new friends at their casual reunions. As if this were not enough, all parishioners of the church in his native district listen to the full story of his moral recovery as announced in the Royal Letter.[56]

Flashbacks mixed occasionally with predictions, especially if the unity of the work stood a more prolonged test. Kmicic did not meet Olenka in the period covered by the four volumes of the novel; but their affair was duly signaled to the readers by occasional hints. Having received the news that the Swedes were in an even worse situation after their victory,

Pan Andrei called to mind at that moment the words of Zagloba, when at their last meeting he said that victories would not improve the Swedish cause, but that one defeat might destroy it. That's a chancellor's head, pondered Kmita, which reads in the future as in a book. Here he remembered the further predictions: how he, Kmita or Babinich, would go to Taurogi, find his Olenka, persuade her, marry her, and have descendants to the glory of the Commonwealth.[57]

Coordinated anticipation and retrospective flashes acted as an additional means of enhancing suspense. They kept interest alive despite the fact that serialization extended reading for many months and, even when occasional links were overlooked, they produced an illusion of continuity.

Naturally, such repetitive passages also performed other esthetic functions. V. Shklovski applied the term "architectonic tautology" to the recurrence of the same episode in a novel, ballad, or folk song, and attributed to this device the same purpose which "verbal tautology"—alliteration, refrain, rhythmical parallelism—fulfill in poetry.[58] Such artful detours twist a straightforward narrative into a whimsical, multistoried edifice. The depicted object is shown on different levels which inevitably delays the climax and serves as a "brake of action."[59]

In serialized novels some authors introduced spectacular collective scenes in which a large number of characters were involved.[60] They clarified the mutual relations among the co-actors and helped to coordinate the elements of the narrative; they provided an opportunity to solve the major problems of the novel in such a way that the solution directly affected the whole party; the effect was comparable to a dress rehearsal. Such scenes appeared in the works of Dickens, and Dostoyevsky used them masterfully in his great works, *Crime and Punishment, The Idiot,* and *The Possessed.*

Sienkiewicz used these collective scenes with moderation. Complicated adventures of his heroes made their simultaneous meetings difficult and rather awkward. Yet he did not disregard this device. Kmicic and his friends gathered at Janusz Radziwill's banquet, to which Olenka and her uncle were also invited; in view of the political decisions of the host the gathering included many other persons. This collective scene determined the situation of all participants for the future. In all three novels, the author arranged a large collective scene at the finale.

Mastery in creating suspense was one of the striking features of the whole *Trilogy*. Despite the considerable length of the separate novels, each produced tension lasting to the very final episode. Incidents of the plot were coordinated in such a way that curiosity never subsided. The novelist did not hesitate to submit the monarchs to mortal dangers. A Swedish detachment attacked the retinue of Casimir returning to his country; a Polish unit trapped the Swedish king. Many other heroes repeatedly experienced fantastic trials. Skrzetuski owed his salvation not only to Chmielnicki's gratitude but also to the Hetman's ruse. Kmicic would have died if Zagloba had not stopped the fighting squad. The author never allowed the readers' interest to wane. If a temporary lull took place, it usually anticipated new dramatic complications and harder trials. Whenever the mood of the narrative brightened, the author staged some theatrical surprise. In *With Fire and Sword* the protagonist talked elatedly about his intention to marry Helena who found a safe refuge in Bar; suddenly an officer entered to announce that Bar had been captured by the Cossacks.[61]

The cumulative effect of anticipation, suspense, and dialogue was demonstrated when Ketling was taken captive by Kmicic's Tartars. Kmicic burned with desire to speak to the prisoner who witnessed Radziwill's courtship of his beloved Olenka.[62] Since the Headquarters subjected Ketling to a detailed inquiry, Kmicic had no opportunity to speak to him, and in the evening he left on a reconnaissance patrol. At last a meeting was arranged, but it was still impossible for Kmicic to obtain the coveted information; no wonder that his patience almost reached the breaking point. The conversation of the friends was not a mere exchange of words but an interplay of contrasting tempers and a means of protracting the suspense.

Minor climaxes were interspersed in the course of the whole

text. The writer conceived fitting conclusions, not only for every volume, but also for separate chapters.[63] Prince Jeremiah spent a sleepless night deliberating whether he should submit himself to the command of other officers or seize power and head the army. In the morning he appeared at the assembly and bluntly declared that he accepted the authority of the vice-Hetmans. And to his statement the author added the words, "a dumb silence dominated the meeting." Sometimes the finales were shaped in such a way that they posed a riddle, and only the following chapter provided a solution. In *With Fire and Sword* the last words of Chapter 15, II, revealed that Jeremiah's army withdrew on the entire front. At the start of the following chapter it turned out that the alleged withdrawal was just a deceptive maneuver.

In *The Deluge*, out of ninety-six chapters about fifty ended with some kind of climax. Sometimes they served as an emotional résumé of the content. At the end of the first chapter, Olenka, asked by her aunt whether she liked Kmicic, embraced her, exclaiming "Oh, my aunt!" The chapters ending with Olenka's prayer (8, III; 8, VI; 15, VI) belonged in the same category. An additional twist was brought about when Olenka decided that she had no right to pray for Kmicic, or when she prayed for Babinicz without realizing that he was identical with Kmicic. Similarly effective were the endings of Chapter 4, V, where after the defeat of the Swedes, the church bells of Jaroslaw rang and the regiments of Czarniecki sang a hymn; Chapter 14, V (also the end of the volume) when Kmicic, went westward and the trees and fields seemed to sing: The Swedes were beaten! Warsaw was taken!; Chapter 12, V, ending with the prayer of King Kazimierz on the eve of the battle for Warsaw; and Chapter 12, III closing with Kmicic's return to his cell after the confession and his subsequent penance.

An opposite effect resulted when after a stormy scene an apparently indifferent remark followed, signaling the return to the normal epic rhythm of life. At the reception (13, I) Janusz Radziwill declared that he joined the Swedes, thereby arousing stormy protests followed by the arrest of the opponents; and Olenka denounced Kmicic, shouting "Go away, traitor!" The last words of the chapter "The banquet was over" provided an anticlimax.

Later (9, II) the Radziwills rejoiced at their successes, but they also received the news that Sapieha was approaching with a powerful army. Prince Janusz dismissed the messenger and "then he fell into deep thought." In another chapter (14, I) he succeeded in convincing Kmicic that a pro-Swedish policy was beneficial to the country and, promising to him a brilliant career, said: "Arise, the future Great Hetman and Governor of Vilno!" And the last words of this chapter were "The dawn appeared in the sky."

The scene in which the Western magnates surrendered to the Swedish king (10, I) ended with the appearance of the jester writing above the door of the city hall the words Mane-Tekel-Fares. And then followed the final sentence closing the chapter: "The sky was covered with clouds, and the storm was approaching."

In a number of cases the end of the chapter coincided with an unexpected turn of events. In Chapter 1, III, Kmicic and his companions sought refuge in a forest, and suddenly a group of soldiers appeared. At this very moment the chapter ended on a note of suspense. In Chapter 17, III, Kmicic was sent to blow up the big Swedish gun while the other officers waited impatiently for the result of his assignment. They heard the explosion, and the chapter concluded with "At last the night began to fade out, but Kmicic did not return to the fortress."[64] Only the following chapter would reveal the full story of this exploit. In a few instances the last episodes of the chapters were curtain effects. When Kmicic, chased by his neighbors, sought refuge in Olenka's manor, she saved his life. Just as soon as the pursuers left, she expelled the man whom she loved saying: "Cain's blood is on your hands! Go away forever!"[65] In 3, VI, Olenka, who just avoided Radziwill's assault, ordered Sakowicz to untie her aunt and sent him to his master. Sometimes the last episodes in the chapters were forecasts of coming events, e.g., 10, III; 1, V; and 4, VI, in which the Swedish king saw a cloud approaching his royal star.

There were cases when Sienkiewicz's technical vigilance apparently slackened. This occurred mainly in the chapters in which the romantic element prevailed. The obvious reason for this was the need of a more relaxed mood, either in view of the content or in order to settle the preliminaries for some major events.

VI *Emotional Chords*

Contrast was one of Sienkiewicz's favorite devices. He liked to interweave the most dramatic events with serene or amusing interludes. For this reason, he made the romance between Skrzetuski and Helena in its early stage so carefree and cheerful. Helena's companionship with Zagloba during the dangerous escape served the same purpose. Likewise, before the military events and after the conflict between Olenka and Kmicic in *The Deluge*, the author inserted an idyllic scene on an estate where Zagloba enjoyed fine liquor and the company of children (11, I). The attempt to kidnap Olenka was preceded by an equally idyllic picture in which Pan Michael, surrounded by Lithuanian beauties, related his impressions of the capital (8, I). Then too, the treason of the Radziwills was exposed during a sumptuous banquet.

Horror, the faithful companion of war, occasionally rose to shocking heights. As a contemporary of the "naturalist school," Sienkiewicz did not approve of its theory, but he did not completely escape its influence. Besides, historical material was not lacking in examples of cruelty.[66] The novelist dutifully reproduced scenes of tortures, lynchings, mass slaughters, and executions. Twice he described appalling impalings.

Occasionally the writer struck stirring notes. In the character of Longinus the novelist amalgamated barbarous, elemental, superhuman power with almost childish naïveté and maidenly tenderness of heart. The warrior behaved bashfully with women, as he vowed to shun them until he had chopped off three pagan heads with one stroke. He fulfilled his vow, only to be slain by Tartar arrows; his death was stylized in the manner of St. Sebastian's martyrdom. Similar moving scenes were brought about by the atmosphere accompanying the last hours of Pan Michael and Ketling. There were a few such moments in the life of Kmicic, particularly when he returned to his estate so seriously wounded that his condition appeared desperate. Moving scenes were associated even more frequently with feminine characters.

Funny characters and entertaining episodes abounded in the *Trilogy*. Pan Michael, an incomparable swordsman, liked to pretend he was a harmless imbecile. His amorous temper contrasted amusingly with his short posture and chronic bad luck in love. The only way to marry him was to behave as Basia did—to propose to him. Rzedzian reconciled devotion to his master with greed, and prudent caution in face of danger with reckless gallantry whenever booty was in store. Old Kiemlicz was a mixture of pretentious pride and voracious avarice. Such funny associations were not limited to the lower classes. Some of Boguslaw Radziwill's actions made even his foes laugh. Zamoyski was certainly amusing when he tried to find decent excuses for his lust. Sapieha, an outstanding statesman and a great patriot, indulgently tolerated the vicious sallies of Zagloba. Such silhouettes and incidents sprinkled throughout the text enriched its fabric and prevented monotony, the greatest potential danger of a serialized novel.

The style and language of the *Trilogy* won unanimous admiration. This approbation was shared even by those critics who disapproved of its content. The author's diction excels as a model of precision and clarity. It appears simple, but this is a kind of simplicity attainable only by genuine masters. The diction never becomes flat, and it is subtly flexible. It is impressive in the carefree passages predominating in the first volume of *Pan Michael* as well as in the gloomiest visions of routs and disasters. It is an essential component in the general polyphony.

As pointed out earlier, many characters were endowed with a specific style which made their identification easy; but all these individual deviations were tightly woven into the fabric of the entire work. Sienkiewicz colored the *Trilogy* with the typical flavoring of the seventeenth century. He skilfully introduced some Latinisms which were common among the gentry both on solemn occasions and in daily speech. He revived various expressions which had long ago become obsolete. The Ukrainian quotations were justly criticized as being inconsistent with the real Ukrainian language, but for the average Pole, Sienkiewicz's mistakes were

[*107*]

imperceptible and did not ruin the effect of an alien language closely related to Polish which the author wished to create.

Some elements of the *Trilogy* posed special difficulties requiring extraordinary mastery of style. This applied to the texts of alleged military orders, manifestoes, messages, political declarations, reports, sermons, occasional speeches, and letters. In several instances real documents were quoted, but a great majority of such passages were composed by Sienkiewicz with consummate skill, creating an impression of authenticity. Kraszewski did not hesitate to write of *With Fire and Sword* that "sometimes the reader feels as if he had read a contemporary memoir, even though the episodes and the main scenes demonstrate a masterful skill and a more sophisticated approach."[67]

The diction of the *Trilogy* maintains a majestic kind of rhythm which is discreet and perceptible in the structure of separate sentences and in the whole sequence of the narrative. Curtin, Sienkiewicz's most zealous translator, was cognizant of this attribute of the work, and he pointed out that his ambition was to render it in English equivalents.[68]

Sienkiewicz did not create a new means of narrative expression, sought no new devices of narrative technique, but he became a master craftsman with the tools already available. Whatever can be said of the historical background of the *Trilogy*, its treatment was colorful, infectious, and impressive. If it is ignored as history, it acquires a refreshed meaning as a legendary vision. The cycle does not reveal any unknown psychological or social aspects of the era, but it introduces a great number of believable characters and persuasive episodes.

The Polish controversy provoked by the *Trilogy* resulted mainly from its message. The opponents reproached the writer for a tendentious presentation of history and for complacency in undermining national vigilance and soundness of judgment. Some critics disapproved of its esthetic qualities. It has often been defined as Sienkiewicz's best achievement and the mainstay of his fame.[69]

CHAPTER 5

Wrestling with the Present

I *Frustrated Genius*

SIENKIEWICZ began to write his first large contemporary novel fifteen months after the completion of the *Trilogy*. At first he called it *In Shackles*. During his work on the novel, he traveled more extensively than his hero. It was begun on July 30, 1889 in Heligoland and continued in Ostend, Zakopane, and Vienna. Before the text was completed in September 1890, he had changed his abode several times.

The *Trilogy* established Sienkiewicz as an author of historical novels. When he abandoned the past, his devoted admirers were surprised and disillusioned. However, even in the *Trilogy* the writer's ties with contemporary problems were an important undercurrent. After its completion some kind of confrontation between the past and the present was inevitable. Whatever sins and errors the ancestors had committed, they left the image of a robust, dynamic society. Were the contemporaries worthy heirs of their predecessors? Were they vigorous enough to face the problems of the modern era?

In his earlier narrative prose, the novelist had demonstrated that he weighed carefully the political and social potential of the peasant class—apparently with a negative result. Now he turned to the privileged class, and his verdict was also severe. In a letter to Janczewska he wrote: "Those who expect that they will find some Jeremiahs, Czarnieckis, etc., will be disappointed, because nowadays there are no such people; but those who like to deliberate on various subjects will find a scope for reflections on the human mind. In brief, one will find there a specimen of a human soul, complex, morbid but true."[1]

The destiny of the upper classes created anxiety as early as the Romantic period. *The Undivine Comedy*, a tragedy by Zygmunt Krasinski,[2] introduced a descendant of an aristocratic family who suffered from deeply rooted skepticism and was afflicted by an egotism which made him incapable of any sincere emotion. This hero was eager to play a spectacular role in the theater of life and treated his fellow men in a detached way, like a poet manipulating words. Many other works in Polish literature contained an equally ominous augury. To his novel on the decaying aristocracy, Kraszewski gave the title *Morituri*.[3] When Sienkiewicz was planning *Without Dogma*, Boleslaw Prus had just published his distinguished novel, *Lalka* (The Doll), in which the aristocratic ways of life were ridiculed.[4]

While introducing his new hero, Sienkiewicz hinted at the symptoms of decadence which he attributed primarily to social causes. In *The Doll* Izabela Lecka, a beauty educated in a hot-house atmosphere of faded aristocracy, lived in an artificial world where everything was arranged to provide comfort and entertainment. She had no contact with ordinary life and was unaware of its troubles and hardships. Similarly in *Without Dogma*, Leon Ploszowski made in his memoirs a significant confession:

. . . generally speaking, all the people of the so-called upper classes do not live a true, real life. Below us something always happens, there is the struggle for life, for bread, a life full of diligent work, animal necessities, appetites, passions, everyday effort,—a palpable life, which roars, leaps, and tumbles like ocean waves, and we are sitting eternally on terraces, discussing art, literature, love, women; strangers to that other life far removed from it, obliterating, out of the seven, the six work-days. Without being conscious of it, our inclinations, nerves, and soul are fit only for holidays. Immersed into blissful dilettantism as in a warm bath, we are half awake, half dreaming. Consuming leisurely our wealth, and our inherited supply of nerves and muscles, we gradually lose our foothold upon the soil.[5]

Equally frustrating was the existence of Ploszowski's father. The son wrote with mild but devastating irony that the old man left in his desk a yellow manuscript about trinity in Nature. This was, of course, a result of the epidemic of intellectual brooding created by Hegel. Leon remembered from this masterpiece only an obscure comparison between the transcendental belief of Christianity in the Father, the Son, and the Holy Spirit, and the natural trinity of oxygen, hydrogen, and ozone, with many other analogous trinities—"a quaint mixture of Hegel and Hoene-Wronski, and utterly useless."[6]

Leon abstained from such intellectual frolics. He was well educated, having earned two university degrees. But his existence remained idle and sterile. Ploszowski's inheritance was sufficient for all possible whims. As to his ambition, it remained dormant. He resided abroad and only visited his homeland occasionally, almost as a foreign guest. Flattery of friends and casual acquaintances surrounded him with a pleasant mist of complacency. In love affairs he was successful without special efforts. He sometimes mused that those people whose parents had become bankrupt were more privileged, because they had an incentive for action developing their energy and will power. Yet even this reflection was subjected to doubt:

I thought sometimes that if I had no means of subsistence I should have to work. Certainly I should have to do something in order to earn my bread; but even then I am firmly convinced that I should not derive the twentieth part of advantage from my capacities. Besides, such men as Darwin or Buckle were rich; Sir John Lubbock is a banker; most of the famous men in France are in easy circumstances. This proves that wealth is not a hindrance, but rather a help towards attaining a proper standing in a chosen field of activity. I confess that as far as I am concerned, it has done me some service as it preserved my character from many a crookedness poverty might have exposed it to.[7]

Ploszowski thought that the "upper classes" were unable to cooperate productively with the rest of the population. He did not believe in any attempt to establish mutual union:

The fact is that between the classes there is a vast gulf that precludes all mutual understanding, and makes simultaneous efforts simply impossible. At least, I look upon it in that light. Sèvres china and common clay,—nothing between; one *très fragile,* the other Ovidius' *"rudis indigestaque moles."* Of course Sèvres china sooner or later breaks, and from the clay the future may mould anything it likes.[8]

Careful education, contacts with intellectuals, and inherited qualities developed in Ploszowski a sophisticated intellect. Excessive self-analysis and introspection and a life of ease deprived him of will power. He claimed that he was not an isolated case but represented a typical state of mind. He often spoke of Slavic unproductiveness, and this label was reminiscent of a long gallery of superfluous men introduced by the Russian writers: Pushkin's Onegin, Lermontov's Pechorin, Turgenev's Rudin and Pavel Kirsanov (*Fathers and Sons*), Goncharov's Oblomov, and Dostoyevsky's Verkhovenski senior (*The Possessed*). However, Ploszowski differed from them by some unique features typical of the end of the century when all traditional beliefs seemed to crumble. He did not feel an urge to support any specific philosophy. Adopting the attitude of an agnostic, he was willing to tolerate a few appearances of piousness if they helped to avoid unpleasantness. This was the way he regarded religion:

Henry the Fourth said Paris was well worth a mass; so say I that the peace of those nearest is worth a mass; people of my class, as a rule, observe religious prescriptions, and I should protest against the outward symbols only in such case, if I could find something more conclusive to say than "I do not know." I go to church because I am a sceptic in regard to my own scepticism.[9]

In view of a long list of predecessors, Ploszowski as an individual deserved only mild curiosity, but as a representative of his era he could stir anxiety. Here was a gifted, educated man, with refined taste, physically healthy, attractive to women—and quite useless. For himself he found the definition "a genius without portfolio," which in his opinion determined perfectly well his state of mind:

I shall take out a patent for the word. But the definition does not apply to me alone. Their name is legion. Side by side with the *improductivité slave* goes a genius without portfolio; it is a pure product of the Slavic soul . . . I do not know another part of the world where so much ability is wasted, in which even those who bring forth something give so little, so incredibly little in comparison with what God had given them.[10]

Was this judgment exaggerated? Chmielowski, a leading critic at the time, fully endorsed it. In his view, there were many such "paraders," capable of affectation and grand gestures but not prepared to assume the burden of everyday work. Chmielowski considered them one of the major calamities of the community.[11]

Owing to the self-consciousness of the hero and his desire to make his memoirs a human document, his diagnosis was given before the plot of the novel began. As so many of his forerunners, the author submitted Ploszowski to the test of love. This was not a mere literary convention. Leon himself attached some hope to the family as an important social element and as a possible augury of regeneration. His friend Sniatynski called him bankrupt but added that his children and grandchildren could become different, and Leon did not object. Sniatynski clarified his view, saying, ". . . to me as a literary man, the community is a dogma; as a private individual, the beloved woman."[12]

Ploszowski was reluctant to part with his freedom; but he met a young woman who satisfied his esthetic criteria and appealed to his sensuality, and he felt irresistibly attracted to her. After the usual hesitation, he intended to propose. News of his father's illness in Rome compelled him to leave. At a distance Anielka's charm lost its fascination, and Ploszowski even had an affair with another woman. When he learned that Anielka, offended by his sudden departure, was to marry another man, he was vexed. At first he did not intervene and even sent his greetings, but his attachment for Anielka was deeper than he realized. Regretting his whims, he asked a friend to persuade her to postpone the wedding; but she had already become Mrs. Kromicki.

Like Goethe's Werther and Pushkin's Onegin, Ploszowski now found Anielka more charming than ever before. He also noticed that she preferred him to her husband, who was a dull and unattractive man. Yet when Leon tried to seduce her, she firmly resisted all his advances. He had to adopt the attitude of a mere friend, which made their mutual relations more tolerable. Anielka's pregnancy did not alter his feelings. Meanwhile, Kromicki went bankrupt and committed suicide. Anielka did not survive the confinement, and Ploszowski followed her by taking his life.

There was some contradiction between the two periods of Ploszowski's romance. In its initial stage, his behavior conformed with his character of a lazy, unscrupulous aristocrat. Things changed after Anielka's wedding. Kromicki did not have the merits of Tatyana's husband in *Eugene Onegin* and aroused no special respect. The competition between the two enamored men was unequal, and the sympathy of the author was in favor of Ploszowski. No really dramatic struggle was in sight. True, the conduct of Ploszowski did not always fall into line with his own esthetic standards, e.g., when he granted Kromicki a loan to strengthen his hold on Anielka; nevertheless, his superiority could not be questioned.

Ploszowski now seemed to regain his youth and vigor, forgetting his former indolence. He no longer looked like a sickly hospital patient. He fought for his rights to happiness; he got rid of any petulance which a smaller man would nurture. The distribution of lights and shades became strangely confused.

At first Ploszowski appeared to be a symptom of a perilous social disease. Later the criticism of the novelist turned not so much against the cynical Don Juan as against the person representing "the Dogma." At one moment the exasperated Leon complained: "Ah me! what a torture to have to deal with virtue, cold and merciless, as the matter of the law!"[13] If this outburst were to be taken seriously, the novel would become a diatribe against the bourgeois prejudices rather than a warning against atheistic agnosticism and intellectual sophistry.

As to the heroine, physical attractiveness and passive charm were her main assets. Her personality lacked sophistication, but this did not make her less tempting in Ploszowski's eyes. Her conduct was erratic. She managed to maintain a risky friendship with Leon and keep him in permanent subservience. If she was guided unswervingly by strict moral standards, why didn't she attempt to part with him?

Some inconsistencies in the novel could be explained at least partly by the ambiguous attitude of the author toward his hero. Sienkiewicz approached his subject as an impartial judge, but occasionally he seemed to identify himself with Ploszowski. This subtle tendency animated the texture of the novel, especially in the final passages of the memoir describing Anielka's death, which may have been partly reminiscent of the writer's own bereavement.

Without Dogma was conceived as a warning and an antidote against the morbid mood of the *fin de siècle*. It turned out that it was the only work acceptable to the growing generation of the "Young Poland." Its herald, Wilhelm Feldman, had some reservations regarding the structure of the novel, but considered it a masterpiece of descriptive psychology. Ploszowski created a fashion, and young bohemians modeled their behavior on his mannerisms.

The novelist attached much hope to the novel and was discouraged by the relatively cool reaction of his Polish readers. He found consolation in the success of *Without Dogma* in other countries. The book was widely read and discussed in Germany and Austria. Tolstoy said to a German interviewer that he liked the novel and that he considered Sienkiewicz to be a great poet; he also stated that *Without Dogma* described a man's love for a woman in a very subtle way.[14] Soon after the publication of the Russian translation, I. Gofshtetter gave a public lecture on Sienkiewicz. He believed that in this novel the Polish author had risen to the level of a literary master by depicting the subtle and intricate psychology of contemporary man.[15] The following year the writer was elected member of the Imperial Academy of Arts and Sciences in Petersburg as expert in the field of psychology and history. For some time, *Without Dogma* was valued primarily for its psychological insight. Later, however, the fascination for the work waned.

II *A Successful Mediocrity*

It was unfortunate for *The Polaniecki Family* that this novel was made available after the publication of *Without Dogma*. Having read the negative assessment of contemporary society, the readers hoped to find in Sienkiewicz's next novel some positive solution. Such anticipation was not the best introduction to *The Polaniecki Family*.

The new protagonist behaved like an impersonation of

the ideals of sober practicality proclaimed in the novelist's youth. Stanislaw Polaniecki, an industrialist, specialized in the dyeing of textiles and was also engaged in commerce. He wished to collect a loan from his distant rural relative, Plawicki. On the latter's estate, Polaniecki met his pretty daughter Marynia, who pleased him so much that he was ready to consider marriage. A financial altercation with the father thwarted the budding romance. Eventually, Plawicki had to sell his estate to a young lawyer, Maszko, and move to Warsaw. In the capital, the young couple had a mutual friend, Litka, a charming twelve-year-old girl who was gravely ill with heart trouble. The precocious child loved Polaniecki but guessed that he was attracted to Marynia. Prior to her death, she made Marynia promise to marry Polaniecki. The wedding took place, and the young pair spent their honeymoon in Italy.

Meanwhile, Polaniecki's firm made huge financial gains, and both he and his partner, Bigiel, became wealthy men. Simultaneously, Maszko, who for some time courted Marynia and ultimately married another woman, went bankrupt, and had to leave town. While Marynia was pregnant, her husband had a brief affair with Mrs. Maszko; afterward he felt even more closely attached to his wife. The childbirth was difficult, but both the infant and the mother survived. The happy husband redeemed Marynia's family estate, and they returned to Krzemien to enter a period of cloudless existence.

The moving love of the teen-aged Litka for Polaniecki filled the best passages of the narrative. It recalled a similar motif in Zola's *Page d'amour;* but Stawar rightly pointed out that the French writer attributed to the girl a sinister role breaking the love of her mother for the doctor, while Litka represented unselfish kindness. Sienkiewicz's novel has been compared with *The Humiliated and Insulted* by Dostoyevsky, where Nelly was equally kind, and although her heart was dedicated to the narrator, she did her best in order to regain for him the love of Natasha Ikhmeneva. In both cases, heart disease precipitated the death of the girl. This was one of the exceptional instances where a definite resemblance could be traced between the respective authors.

Sienkiewicz himself hinted at a relationship between *Without Dogma* and *The Polaniecki Family.* Many characters in *The Polaniecki Family* were acquainted with the "genius without portfolio" and his relatives. The news of Ploszowski's suicide reached Polaniecki and his friends, and they deplored the loss. Obviously, the incidents in both works belonged to about the same period.

Polaniecki conceded that in some respects he was inferior to Ploszowski. He realized that he was less refined and made of rougher stuff but intimated that the trials of life made toughness an advantage. Above all, Polaniecki considered himself a man of action, while Ploszowski was a specimen suitable for a display case.

As to moral principles, there was no essential difference between the two men. In his business affairs Polaniecki was practical and tended to ignore ethical scruples. His most profitable commercial deal was due to a bad harvest and an expected famine in Russia. Having received this vital news before the other merchants, he shrewdly realized its commercial potential. He bought up great quantities of grain in advance and when prices soared made an excellent profit. The fact that he owed this gain to human misery simply never entered his mind. He also lacked rigid rules in sexual affairs. His involvement with Mrs. Maszko did not impair his marital life, and he dismissed the affair as trivial. Such an indulgent approach radically differed from the contemporary writings of Paul Bourget, whose novel *La terre promise* (1892), demonstrated the painful consequences of a lighthearted love affair: Francis Nayrac had to abandon his fiancée and take care of his daughter without ever tasting the bliss of parenthood.

In religious matters, Polaniecki also closely resembled the opportunist Leon. His faith was practically nonexistent; he began to value religion owing to his association with Marynia. His wife regularly attended church services and faithfully adhered to the duties prescribed by the catechism. Her religion was formal, but it contributed to her happiness, comfort, and peace of mind. Under her influence, Polaniecki admitted that an indulgent attitude toward religion made life easier. During his stay in Rome, he reasoned that he would be an arrogant fool if he sought his own forms of worship and love rather than accepting those which had been confirmed by the test of two thousand years. In Polaniecki's mind religion was basically a matter of convenience and comfort.

In view of these analogies, one could hardly see Ploszowski and Polaniecki as contrasting characters. They possessed too many features in common. However, Polaniecki's greater vitality, lack of morbid introspection, and practical approach to current problems made him outwardly a different man. Although he occasionally stumbled, he succeeded in establishing a family and making it happy. His objectives were modest and within his reach. The sterner school of life was his source of education.

Occasionally Polaniecki realized that his world was too narrow and that there were other goals besides making money; but being a sober man he did not want to abandon tangible and accessible successes for the sake of undetermined phantoms. He was also more representative of his community. Chmielowski pointed out that, although there were many men like Ploszowski, they were undoubtedly in the minority, while the Polanieckis were plentiful everywhere.[16]

The author could adopt one of three attitudes toward his protagonist. He could treat him as an exponent of the Positivist values which he wanted to promulgate. Another possibility was a purely realistic approach without any didactic recommendations. Finally, the novelist could express some disapproval; a touch of satirical irony would create a distance between his own opinions and his portrait. This happened in the case of Jozef Weyssenhof's novel *The Life and Thoughts of Zygmunt Podfilipski* (1898), which would have appeared an inferior work, if it had been taken seriously; fortunately, the novel gained refreshing vigor owing to an ironic flavoring.

If the first alternative is considered, *The Polaniecki Family* becomes provocatively degrading. Whatever can be said of Polaniecki, he was not properly equipped for the role of an ideal. Under certain conditions, such people could be tolerated, but they could not be recommended as models. There was nothing in the protagonist to kindle worship or admiration, and he some-times looked like an anti-hero.[17] In this case, the serialization of the novel became a definite handicap, as the novelist could see the work in its entirety only after its completion.

From the esthetic point of view, it would be tempting to sup-pose that there was no ground for identifying the author's opin-ions with the conduct of his characters. His correspondence does not confirm such a distinction. However, Sienkiewicz seemed to attach less significance to *The Polaniecki Family* than to his other works. He even spoke more warmly of his minor writings such as "From the Memoirs of a Poznan Tutor."

Of his contemporaries, Chmielowski's analysis of the novel emphasized the ironic approach, noticeable in the shaping of the plot. This was probably the reason why one of the American translators of *The Polaniecki Family* published the book under the title *The Irony of Life*. Naturally, such a title intimated some emo-tional distance between the author and his material.[18] Significantly enough, Curtin also gave it a different title—*Children of the Soil*—which hinted at the ultimate recovery of the Krzemien estate by Polaniecki. In both cases the name of the main character was rec-ognized as an improper definition of the writer's message.

Whatever the author thought of his hero, it did not diminish the value of the book as a diagnostic probe. Having dissociated himself from the lower and higher strata, Sienkiewicz now turned to the middle class as a potential source of strength, and his verdict was more encouraging. Here at last something con-structive was apparently underway. Factories and workshops thrived; wealth increased; estates were saved from foreign pur-chasers and reckless native gamblers; and family bonds remained as sound as ever, constituting a reliable mainstay of the social structure. Moral standards did not look impressive, but at least some outward decency was maintained. Religion was formal and superficial but exerted a favorable influence on everyday life and safeguarded family life from destructive decadence. Such is a purposely simplified portrait of society which may be deduced from the novel. It is mildly optimistic, but it lacks enthusiasm. The author felt closer to the Ploszowskis and to the intellectual bohemians of his short stories than to the self-satisfied businessmen.

As is habitual in literary works and invariably true in Sienkiewicz's writings, his negative characters are artistically superior to his positive figures. This applies principally to the persons participating in a marginal plot, which adds some piquancy to the novel, seemingly referring to the writer's painful experiences in his unfortunate second marriage. In a number of his letters to friends, Sienkiewicz emphatically stated that the novel had nothing in common with his personal troubles, but his contemporaries thought otherwise.

The marginal episode deals with the story of a talented poet, Zawilowski, destroyed by the hypocrisy of the drawing rooms. A beautiful young lady, Lineta Castelli, agreed to become his fiancée but later found out that she preferred another young man, stupid but handsome. She was tired of playing an embarrassing role before her intelligent suitor: "More and more often it happened that waking up in the morning and thinking of a prospective meeting with her fiancé and the need to tune up to his high pitch, she felt like a child expecting a difficult lesson."[19] She relaxed with the dull Kopowski, who amused her and did not require any highbrow conversation. In the subsequent intrigue, Lineta's aunt, Mrs. Bronicz, played an outstanding role. She always supported her niece with insolent sophistry and defended her as a victim of alleged mental cruelty.

When the poet learned of Lineta's elopement with Kopowski, he was beside himself. Mrs. Bronicz provided the last straw when (in her letter) she attributed to Zawilowski the exclusive responsibility for the whole incident. The helpless young man attempted suicide. It turned out that his wound was not fatal but his genius faded away. The analogy with the author's own life was but thinly veiled.

A few other artists and intellectuals appeared in the novel. The painter Swirski occasionally expressed the author's opinions. Some figures belonging to high society pretended to have a knowledge of the arts. They joined the bohemians in order to enhance their position in society. Miss Castelli considered herself a painter. Another fine character in the novel was Mr. Plawicki, Marynia's father, an inveterate idler, a pompous and pathetic fool, fond of solemn phraseology, and a sybarite feigning patriarchal homeliness. He appeared chiefly at the beginning of the novel and was quite amusing.[20]

As a potential program, *The Polaniecki Family* met with sharp disapproval. As a depiction of society it had some merit which became more visible in the distant perspective; naturally it was a one-sided picture. The Russian critic Chernyshevsky coined the derogatory term "Oblomovschina" from the character of Oblomov in the novel by Goncharov. In the same way some Polish critics used the word *Polaniecczyzna*, which became almost a battle cry in the campaign against the bourgeois mold—and against Sienkiewicz.

The novel contains features of expert craftsmanship. The introductory chapters create interest and skillfully begin the plot. Later the structure becomes more confused, but it does not lack cohesion. Even the story of Lineta Castelli is coordinated with the other episodes in a satisfactory way.

From the indifferent material which served as a social background, the author peeled off a number of characters who aroused surprise, protest, or even indignation. This sharp reaction indicated that there was some truth in them and that they were not cardboard creations but reflections of reality. The dialogue, characterization, and the narrative at times bore the author's qualities of clarity and precision, both attributes of Sienkiewicz's mature writings.

The reception of *The Polaniecki Family* abroad was more favorable, especially in the West. In Einsiedeln, Switzerland, where a competition was held for the best novel, out of 678 participants, 311 voted for this novel, while the remaining votes were widely scattered. And in America William Morton Payne (*Dial*, July 1, 1895, pp. 20-21) reviewed the work with respectful approbation:

The strength of the book is in its entire sanity, its freedom from exaggeration of sensationalism, and its psychological insight. It must be reckoned among the finer fiction of our time, and shows its author to be almost as great a master in the field of the domestic novel as he had previously been shown to be in that of imaginative historical romance.

III *Mists of a Revolt*

Once again the novelist resumed his wrestling with contemporary problems, following the events of 1905. During the Russo-Japanese War, the revolutionary underground in Russia came out into the open. Radical Poles abandoned the policy of passive obedience; the Socialists began a struggle which manifested itself in mass demonstrations and armed action against the Russian regime. Sienkiewicz observed these developments with apprehension. He feared that the revolutionary doctrine would overshadow patriotism and that violence would undermine moral and religious principles. Above all, he disapproved of a possible split in the community into antagonistic factions competing with each other and thwarting a concentrated effort in support of a common cause. This was the background of Sienkiewicz's last contemporary novel, *Wiry* (Whirlpools). He began to publish it in March 1908; the last installments appeared in April 1910.

The new novel belonged to the flourishing anti-revolutionary literature. This kind of writing had been formed in Russia where some writers joined in a campaign against the "nihilists" in the 1860's. The reaction produced such works as Turgenev's *Fathers and Sons,* Goncharov's *The Precipice,* Dostoyevsky's *The Possessed,* as well as a number of other tales by lesser authors. A. F. Pisemski published a novel called *V vodovorote* (In the Whirlpool), anticipating the title used by the Polish writer.[21] Some typical motifs appeared independently in different works, e.g., scenes of reckless and unnecessary assaults and suicides of the revolutionary leaders. At that time the Poles were involved in an open armed rising.

Since he only had indirect contact with the fighting revolutionaries, Sienkiewicz's knowledge of the background material was one-sided. The author did not take part in any activity which would have provided him with firsthand information about the revolutionary camp and its activities. The available data were not quite reliable, but the theme appeared urgent and caused considerable anxiety. Prus also wrote an anti-revolutionary novel entitled *Dzieci* (The Children). Once again Sienkiewicz competed with his good friend.

At the beginning of *Whirlpools,* attention centered around the last will of an old squire, Zurowski, who disinherited his family and bequeathed his estate to an agricultural school. His relatives were reluctant to accept the will but reconciled themselves to the situation. Although Zurowski stipulated that among the candidates to the school priority would be granted to the peasants' sons, the interested people would have preferred that the property be divided among the local farmers. Obviously the writer was still not convinced that the social consciousness of the peasant class had made enough progress. However, he noticed important changes which constituted a good omen: "The Dabrowski March which had been a slogan for one hundred thousand people, now appeals to millions." This remark expressed the quintessence of the novelist's hope for the future.

His estimate of the contemporary gentry was still unfavorable. In addition to other faults, servility became more widespread than in the past. Using Gronski as a mouthpiece, the author expressed his opinion on possible cooperation with the Russians as follows:

The realists want to rely on this very Reality which, however, does not want to reckon with them, or with anyone else. Let us suppose that the name of their party is Peter and that this Peter addresses himself, quite sincerely, to Reality and speaks to it: "Listen, maiden! I am ready to recognize thee and even to fall in love with thee but allow me for some time to stand on my own legs, to rest, and to stretch my aching bones." And Reality replies to him with an Uralian kindness, "Peter Petrovich! You miss the point, so I deprive you of the right to speak. It does not matter whether you love me or not; you must unbutton and take off a certain part of your clothing, which incidentally may become useful to me, and lie down on this bench; as to the rest, do trust my strength and my whip." If some realist listens to this story, he may object but inwardly he would admit that I am right and that such is a real picture of the situation.[22]

As to socialism, the novelist considered it alien to the national character, and pointed out that the doctrine was imported from the outside. At any rate, society was not yet ripe for a revolutionary change. The armed attacks were haphazard, and the victims often innocent persons inspired by the best possible intentions. The situation was even worse when crowds appeared in the streets, as their behavior was quite unpredictable. This harsh judgment of the revolutionary group was not convincingly substantiated. The only representative of the revolutionaries introduced in the novel was a young student who frankly called himself a third-rate agent of his party. In addition to the student, the author mentioned some anonymous and obscure agents responsible for reckless assault. The reader was never given a chance of getting acquainted with the more important leaders of the movement.

Into this political turmoil the author inserted two individual plots. An attractive nobleman, Krzycki, fell in love with a charming young lady. She was of Polish extraction, but was adopted by an English industrialist and inherited his wealth. She seemed to like the squire. It turned out that the lady was at one time a local peasant girl who was seduced by her suitor when she was but sixteen. Betrothal followed, and the squire behaved insolently, offending his fiancée so deeply that she broke the engagement. The author intimated that the fantastic career of the young lady in England made her practically unrecognizable. As to her misadventure in early youth, it deserved comparison with a minor episode in *The Polaniecki Family*. Its main actor was Gontowski, a poor squire who for some time had high hopes of marrying Marynia and even defended her honor. This did not prevent him from having affairs with peasant beauties. One of them greeted him in Krzemien where he arrived as a guest:

Meanwhile Gontovski came and having hung his overcoat on a peg in the entrance, he was looking in it for a handkerchief, when by a strange chance Rozulka, young Stas' nurse, found herself also in the entrance and approaching Gontovski embraced his knees, and then kissed his hands.

"Oh! how art thou, how art thou? What wilt thou say?" asked the heir of Yalbrykov.

"Nothing! I only wished to make obeisance," said Rozulka submissively.

Gontovski bent a little to one side, and began to search for something with his fingers in his breast pockets; but evidently she had come only to bow to the squire, for, without waiting for a gift, she kissed his hand again, and walked away quietly to the nursery.

Gontovski went with a heavy face to the rest of the company, muttering to himself in bass,

"Um–dee–dree! Um–dree dree! Um–dramta ta!"[23]

This charming encounter indicated that the relations between the squire and his subordinates portrayed in the earlier novel were still quite feudal. In *Whirlpools* the relations were almost reversed. The former peasant girl belonged to high society on an equal footing and was responsible for the cancellation of the betrothal.

The central figure of another plot was the student Laskowicz who was employed as tutor on an estate. He abandoned his post and devoted himself wholeheartedly to revolutionary activity. He was hopelessly in love with a talented violinist. In Warsaw he found himself in trouble, and the police were tracing him. He owed his escape to the help of some members of the gentry and to a clever servant girl, one of the well-drawn feminine characters. The mob, stirred by Laskowicz, murdered the violinist on the eve of her concert, which had been organized to aid victims of famine. Laskowicz felt responsible for her death and committed suicide.

The symptoms of social disintegration were viewed with pessimism. One of the characters, Swidnicki, in a tirade which referred to the title of the novel, made a clean breast of his desperate foreboding:

Listen to the atheist, or at least a man who has nothing in common with religion. Enlightenment without religion will breed only thieves and bandits . . . we are hopelessly lost. There are only whirlpools in our country . . . And they are not whirlpools on the deep water where there is the peaceful depth below—but whirlpools of sand. Now a storm blows from the East and the sterile sand covers our tradition, civilization, culture—the whole Poland and turns it into a desert in which flowers perish and only jackals can survive.[24]

In spite of its shortcomings, the novel presented a varied

picture of the community. *Whirlpools* included many sharp exchanges of opinion attesting to the author's desire to express the views of opposing camps. Although the author's sympathies were quite clear, his mouthpiece Gronski did not belong to any party.

Social conflicts prevailed in the narrative, but the writer also included a number of schemes typical of novels of adventure. One of the main characters was seriously wounded; another fell victim of a mob. Execution of the party verdict, preparation of a manor for an expected siege by the revolutionaries, assault in a forest, clashes with the police, escapes—these were a few episodes contained in the tale. The main love affair did not follow the usual pattern of a literary romance and demonstrated the author's eagerness to keep in step with the times.

The same tendency was apparent in the style. When the "Moonlight Sonata" was played, Gronski, "who had a poet's imagination and a powerful gift of changing acoustic sensations in a vision, half closed his eyes and began to weave it out of his soul."[25] The subsequent attempt to translate music into visual dreams and words hardly could have appeared in any of Sienkiewicz's earlier works. Another display of the modernist taste was the student's letter to his beloved, which was a transparent parody of the mannerisms practiced by Przybyszewski and his followers:

One night I called you, but you did not hear me and did not come. Now I stretch again my arms towards you and say, "Come and fall asleep on my heart."

"And when the time of awakening comes, I will wake you for the brief moments of delights which love gives and for endless labor demanded by the Idea."

"For labor and perhaps for martyrdom!"

"But there is more happiness in the martyrdom for the new dawns of life than in the darkness, stench, ashes, and mildew of the graves."

"So come, even for martyrdom."

"And until our lives melt in the sea of nothingness, stay with me."

"Oh my beloved one!"[26]

CHAPTER 6

Feasts and Catacombs

I The Vision of Rome

BESIDES "Wyrok Zeusa" (The Verdict of Zeus, 1890), the story "Let Us Follow Him" (1892) heralded Sienkiewicz's new interest in the ancient world. The author's fondness for antiquity began early in his youth. Later he acquired the habit of regularly reading the ancient classics. Once he competed with Jeremiah Curtin in quoting the verses of Horace. His frequent journeys to Italy and a trip to Greece helped him to gain a sound knowledge of the ancient *realia*. In the spring of 1894, he conceived the idea of writing a long novel on early Christianity. The serialization of *Quo Vadis?* began the following year.

Literary works based on the history of the Roman Empire were quite plentiful. Some of them coincided with the growing interest in the origin of Christianity during the Romantic period. Zygmunt Krasinski's tragedy, *Iridion* (1836), introduced a Greek rebel who tried to turn the Christian dissenters against Rome. *The Last Days of Pompeii* (1834) by Edward Bulwer Lytton was available in Polish and was widely read. Even more popular was *Fabiola* (1854) by Nicholas Wiseman, which was twice translated into Polish and reprinted several times.

Other more renowned works on similar themes were: John Henry Newman's *Callista,* Paul Bereille's *Emilie,* Hermann Geiger's *Lydia,* George J. Whyte-Melville's *The Gladiators,* René du Mesnil Marincourt's *Vivia, ou les Martyrs,* and F. N. Farrar's *Darkness and Dawn, a Story of Nero's Days,* as well as two Polish novels *Caprea and Roma* (1860) and *Nero's Rome* (1866) by Jozef I. Kraszewski.

In both Italy and France, the theme of Nero was a great

favorite.[1] Sienkiewicz was probably acquainted with the novel *Acté* by Alexandre Dumas but did not remember it well, as once he called it a drama by mistake. In *Le martyre de Saint Saturnin* by Soulié, one of the characters, Cilo, although he is not a Greek, reminds one of Chilo in *Quo Vadis?* The novel of Agostino della Spada, *Mondo antico,* published in two volumes in 1877, remained almost unnoticed; later its author pretended that his work exerted some influence on Sienkiewicz's *Quo Vadis?* From the beginning of the seventeenth century some thirty-nine Italian plays were written about Nero, according to F. Giannini.[2] *Salammbô* by Gustave Flaubert (1862) had no direct connection with the background of *Quo Vadis?* but it became a model for historical novels based on antiquity and served as an example of the conscientious treatment of all material available. In Flaubert's novel, as in *Quo Vadis?*, the two outstanding episodes of the narrative are a magnificent banquet and a slaughter of real or avowed enemies.

The Polish novelist relied basically on the historical works of ancient writers, such as Tacitus and Suetonius. Likewise, he knew some studies of modern historians. He was aquainted with the works of Charles Ernest Beulé, Fustel de Coulanges, Allard, Baudrillart, and Gaston Boissier. Unlike Chateaubriand in *Les Martyrs,* he avoided the miraculous occurrences which appeared so frequently in the French work. He used every opportunity to enhance his knowledge of the period. From one of his friends, he learned of an essay by Kazimierz Morawski on Petronius Arbiter.[3] He was indebted to *The History of the Origin of Christianity* (1873) by Ernest Renan, especially to the fourth book "The Antichrist."

The setting of the novel was prepared with utmost care. The author's numerous visits to various parts of Italy where the plot of *Quo Vadis?* would take place were not in vain. He frequented the museums to learn as much as possible about Roman customs, religious rites, dwellings, food, clothing, jewels, arts, superstitions, tastes, entertainments, occupations, and all those aspects that made up the Roman way of life. The writer had an excellent command of the necessary terminology and used it correctly whenever he wanted to underscore the local or historical coloring.

The author thoroughly assimilated this rich collection of material. He depicted many aspects of ancient Rome, embracing various social levels. He felt equally at ease in the narrow lanes crowded by Roman artisans and merchants and in the palace of the emperor. As an attempt to create the spirit of antiquity, the novel met with unanimous acclaim. Professor Tadeusz Zielinski, a celebrated expert on ancient culture, overheard at one of his seminars at Warsaw University a derogatory remark concerning *Quo Vadis?* The noted scholar protested.[4] In Zielinski's opinion, the portrait of Rome painted by Sienkiewicz was perfectly accurate and reliable. Every detail corresponded with the available data with but one exception, the mention of coffins in which early Christians were buried. (This form of burial did not appear until the Middle Ages.)

The political aspect of the plot concentrated on the intrigues and entertainments at the Imperial Court, and culminated in the burning of the capital and the succeeding persecution of the Christians. The selection of incidents served to dramatize the destiny of the main characters, but it left some important questions unanswered. One may wonder how it was possible for the Roman Empire to exert such a powerful influence over the whole ancient world if all its outstanding statesmen indulged mainly in mutual antagonisms and rivalry for Imperial grace. After all, the *Pax Romana* lasted for another three hundred years and brought to the Roman Empire periods of brilliant political and military triumphs.

Of course the court of Nero did not represent the whole of Roman society. Even among the courtiers there were people who had been excellent warriors (Vinitius) or administrators (Petronius). However, only relics of the ancient *virtus Romana* survived; people like Plautius and his wife Pomponia Graecina had to live in obscurity and eternal anxiety. Such incongruities in Roman life made speedy expansion of the Christian faith more plausible.

In the opening chapters the novel suggested that the pagan world portrayed in *Quo Vadis?* was doomed and its days were numbered, that it lacked guiding principles, faith and morality, and that it practiced vulgar hedonism. Yet the author attributed to this accursed Rome glamor and magnificence. Even the obnoxious Nero was not an exception. When Lygia heard him singing at the banquet, she found him almost attractive in his laurel wreath and she thought his hymn to Venus quite beautiful.

Of course, Nero had many repulsive vices. His self-centered conceit made him a foolish buffoon; his absolute lack of moral principles was subhuman; his lack of individual taste contradicted his ambition to become a truly great artist. When at the banquet some of the courtiers praised his poem, limitless vanity appeared in his face, not only bordering on stupidity, but identical with it.

Yet in one moment at least Nero showed himself in a different light. He happened to sing his hymn to Venus really well, so that he impressed his listeners. He felt a sincere emotion and did not want to listen to the usual eulogies. When Petronius said that he admired the poem, Nero replied to him in a surprisingly sensible way; "I know. You are too lazy to force yourself to praises. And you are sincere like Tullius Senecio, but you are a better connoisseur than he." He pointed out that he was more self-conscious than his court thought: "Do you think that I am blind or unreasonable? . . . They have made me believe in my cruelty, so that sometimes I ask myself if I am not cruel . . . But they do not understand that the man's deeds sometimes may be cruel, but he may not be cruel . . . Oh, nobody, even you, my dear, will believe that sometimes, when music lulls my spirit, I feel so good as a baby in a cradle."[5]

Nero looked like a different man in this peculiar mood. He spoke kindly of other musicians. He agreed to the marriage of Vinitius with Lygia and presently exclaimed: "Oh, how nice it is to make other people happy! I would not like to do anything else in my whole life." For a while it seemed that, after all, art successfully replaced moral principles. Nero began to resemble Sienkiewicz's contemporaries, like Oscar Wilde who proclaimed art for art's sake and raised it to the rank of the supreme human value. Yet it would be wrong to overestimate this brief incident. After all, it occurred immediately before the conflagration of Rome, and for this reason it appeared like a device for producing a theatrical effect. This was one of the drawbacks of the author's technical virtuosity; it could arouse distrust.

Petronius dominated the novel from the beginning to the end. This prominence he owed not only to his character but also to his association with the author's deeply rooted sympathies. He was comparable to Ploszowski, except that in *Quo Vadis?* Sienkiewicz did not allow his didactic tendency to mar his fine portrait. The significance of Petronius was assessed by one of the earliest American critics of the novel:

So we have the nineteenth century embodied in Petronius Arbiter, with the transcendent alchemy of imagination by which a great student of the first century and the nineteenth century can at will invest himself with either. The shadow of a name behind the *Satyricon* could not, as his critics suppose, be a figure so delicate, so indifferent, so subtle, and so strong with whom we are so much at home in the scenes of *Quo Vadis?* He is a perfect host; we sit with him at his table enchanted by the genial cynicism as if he were a friend, though he professes no faith in friendship. We can complain of the 'divine' Nero certain that the courtier will not betray us; we can speak with reverence of the gods, sure that this sceptic will respect us. He is a perfect gentleman, this Epicurean created by the only imagination moulded in the Catholic belief, expanded by Catholic heroism, pruned of extravagance by Catholic moralities. The author's soul has gone into this creation. His own passionate, Polish Catholic heart beats in the equable pulsations of Petronius. . . . In him he vivifies his own hopes and disappointments, his speculative difficulties, his social and religious creeds . . .[6]

Occasionally, Petronius looked indeed like the author's stylized self-portrait. Not unexpectedly, his guiding principle was neither religious nor moral but esthetic. In this respect there was an apparent affinity between him and Nero. In the case of Petronius the cult of beauty was not contaminated with baseness. It was associated with a brilliant mind and a sense of dignity. At the Imperial Court he succeeded in maintaining moderation in corruption and safeguarded his own independent way of life. Petronius had courage enough to apply his esthetic criteria not just to the arts but to his whole conduct.

It would be erroneous to assume that such a character, seemingly the product of a preconceived notion, would have to become lifeless and artificial. The author made him a gambler who enjoyed a dangerous game and was unwilling to deprive himself of the resulting thrills. For this reason, he occasionally risked his own life by doing things which submitted him to mortal danger. His laziness conformed with his philosophy. He would be reluctant to spoil the blissful harmony of godlike existence by reckless bustle. Petronius could withstand the fury of the mob threatening Caesar after the burning of Rome. But he would not tolerate a single drunkard behaving insolently and smelling of liquor; he coolly killed him with his short sword and then resumed the interrupted conversation as if nothing had happened.

Petronius represented a refined facet of ancient culture. His composure was revealed almost at the very beginning of the novel. The patrician sympathized with Vinitius in his amorous difficulties, but advised him to behave sensibly, thus revealing his own fondness of comfort:

"Calm thyself, mad descendant of consuls. We do not lead the barbarians bound behind our cars, to make wives of their daughters. Beware of the extremes. Exhaust simple, honorable methods and give thyself and me time for meditation. Chrysothemis seemed to me too a daughter of Jove, and still I did not marry her, as Nero did not marry Acte, though they called her a daughter of King Attalus."[7]

Serene skepticism permitted Petronius, like Ploszowski, to tolerate all creeds and philosophies without accepting any one of them. He even considered the Christian teachings objectively and recognized their advantages, but he would not part with the surroundings to which he was fondly attached. Ironically, this agnostic lost the struggle with Tigellinus because he defended the Christians. His death acquired a potential symbolic significance.

Chilo Chilonides appeared as an inevitable by-product of the same civilization which established the greatness and splendor of Greece and Rome. He was an amusing mixture of Thersites and the ubiquitous Figaro, the Greek sophists and Zagloba. Occasionally he resembled Petronius; both understood each other well and readily found a common language. In his letter to Vinitius, Petronius frankly admitted: ". . . sometimes it seems to me that I am just like this Chilo, not in the least better than he." The difference between them depended mainly on the external conditions. The same lack of scruples which in Petronius's case was not deprived of charm became repulsive when it was degraded to the vulgar struggle for survival. Taught to tolerate all kinds of humiliation, Chilo remained invariably entertaining and occasionally used his wit as a weapon of revenge:

"Well," said he, "which means have you got for this?" "You have got the means, my lord; I have only the wit." "So you will be a donkey which conquers the fortress with the sacks of gold?" "I am only a poor philosopher," humbly replied Chilo, "and you possess gold."[8]

One of the controversial psychological problems was Chilo's conversion. Various critics found it unconvincing. The same doubts could be applied to a greater extent to Vinitius. The story of his romance did not provide a sufficient reason for his spiritual transformation. As to Lygia, she resembled other women in Sienkiewicz' novels, whose main advantage was passive resistance.

To do justice to the author, *Quo Vadis?* should be viewed on a comparative scale. In *Fabiola* by Cardinal Wiseman, Pancratius declaimed: "Eagerly have I watched in thee the opening germ of each Christian virtue and thanked God as it appeared. I have noted thy docility, thy gentleness, thy piety, and thy love of God and man. I have seen with joy thy lively faith, and thy indifference to worldly things and thy tenderness to the poor."[9] Vinitius was also enchanted when he met Lygia for the first time, but for different reasons; he saw her naked, bathing at the fountain in the garden.

II *The Controversial Message*

The collective vision of pagan Rome dazzled the reader with its resplendency. Against such a background the Christians paled by comparison, and when they appeared as a collective body, they were anticlimactic. They oozed kindness and love, but they lacked the fascination of their pagan counterparts. Peter and Paul repeated the teachings of the Gospel in a dignified and reasonable way, but personally they were inconspicuous and resembled conventional portraits of the saints. Of course, the sources regarding the early Christians were scarcer than the documentation available on the pagans; but *Quo Vadis?* was a work of fiction, not a historical treatise. Sienkiewicz's own views on the historical novel authorized him to seek the missing links in his own imagination. It was also argued that the dimmer vision of the Christian world harmonized with its guiding principles of self-denial and humility. Similarly in the third part of his *Forefathers' Eve*, Mickiewicz introduced Father Peter as an insignificant monk, mechanically repeating the orthodox words of prayers and rites, who nevertheless was spiritually superior to the great poet Konrad. Yet if such artistic solutions were adopted as a general rule, the great painters should have been impelled to show Christian figures pale and colorless.

Some critics argued that the life of the pagans was external and that the life of the Christians was centered in their souls. In view of this, a different method had to be adopted in painting the pictures of the two worlds. Christian episodes had primarily emotional value; they took place in the cemetery and in the catacombs where lights were dim and people looked ethereal and hazy. As a result, a mystic halo surrounded Christian Rome while the pagans appeared in full light.[10]

The affinity of *Quo Vadis?* with the earlier works of the novelist was evident. His frustrating estimate of the present induced him to seek the eternal truths. Prus in *The Pharaoh* tried to demonstrate that some current problems were as old as the Egyptian civilization and that the rules guiding the behavior of mankind remained unchanged. Sienkiewicz believed that there was an analogy between the dissolution and moral chaos of his own epoch, and the Rome of the pre-Christian era. He wanted to show that the same expedient which had revived the ancient world contained hope and promise for his generation.

This tendency in *Quo Vadis?* did not weigh too heavily on the individual episodes, as it resulted from the general sequence of incidents. The power of Rome was a delusion. The paradise of Petronius was collapsing. No happiness was in store for Vinitius and Lygia outside Christianity. One of the ideas given special

[*134*]

emphasis was the view that Christianity was not hostile to earthly enjoyment and that it should not be identified with asceticism.

The novel met the widespread approval of the Christian communities. The Pope bestowed his blessing upon the author. There were, however, some discordant voices. Soon after the publication of the Italian translation of *Quo Vadis?*, two clerics expressed diametrically contrasting opinions about its moral value. Antonio Pavissich, a Jesuit, condemmed the novel, classifying it as morbid art. On the other hand, a celebrated preacher, Father Giovanni Semerianni, in a public lecture published in 1900 defined *Quo Vadis?* as an apologetic work written in defense of Christianity. This controversy was resumed on various occasions by other authors. Recently, Alfons Bronarski reviewed the verdicts of his predecessors and came to the conclusion that the novel was a Christian work.[11]

A slightly different problem was raised by a few contemporary authors in Poland. Konrad Gorski, examining the message of the novel, stated bluntly: "Such a vision of Christianity and such an opposition between a declining ancient culture and the birth of a new Christian one, as Sienkiewicz had presented in *Quo Vadis?*, cannot suffice today. Everybody feels that Sienkiewicz officially is on St. Paul's side but Petronius is closer to his heart." The polemics on this subject have not ceased.[12]

As to the image of the early Christians, Marucchi, and more recently Dobraczynski,[13] noticed more discrepancies between the text of the novel and present historical data. Naturally, Sienkiewicz could not have considered information which had not been available during his work on the novel. Some of the omissions in the description of the Christian rites were due to the author's privilege to select.

There were also attempts to interpret *Quo Vadis?* as a revolutionary work. An article printed in the Polish Socialist daily, *Naprzod* (Forward, 1897), suggested that the main theme of the novel was a campaign against the tyrant Nero living in gold and lust and maltreating the silent crowd of slaves.[14] Notwithstanding the cool treatment of *Quo Vadis?* by other Communist critics, I. K. Gorsky set forward the vision of the decay at the top in pagan Rome and the opposition of the Christians against imperial dictatorship. In his opinion, the greatest value of this "Christian epic" consisted in showing the process of social persecutions, comparable to the modern rule of violence and injustice. Sienkiewicz did not idealize the Roman "Lumpenproletariat" but demonstrated that even though the plebians were corrupted, they would not reconcile themselves indefinitely with the monstrous abuses of the ruling clique. Growth of national protest increasing the influence of Christians on the sound elements of the community resulted in the inevitable peril for the Roman Empire.[15]

Naturally, the novel was also viewed as an allegory pointing to the situation of the author's native land and its imminent liberation. Callina-Lygia and Ursus belonged to the tribe of Lygians who allegedly were the ancestors of the Poles. The miraculous rescue of Lygia from the cruelty of Nero contained obvious implications.

It was the Christian message in *Quo Vadis?* which was responsible for its widespread acclaim. With his customary intuition of the current atmosphere, Sienkiewicz wrote and published this novel at the most opportune moment. At the end of the nineteenth century there was some feeling of general anxiety comparable to the premonitions and fears at the end of the first millennium. The good news announced by the novelist brought a feeling of optimism which was eagerly awaited. This effect was most vigorous in France, where the date of the French translation coincided precisely with the very end of the stormy nineteenth century. On the other hand, some sophisticated readers resented the theme chosen by the author. In England, a noted critic, favorably disposed to Sienkiewicz on account of his *Trilogy*, was so strongly prejudiced against the novel that he had no desire to read it:

If I have not read *Quo Vadis?*, it is partly because life is short, and partly because I have an invincible dislike to stories written for the purpose of "contrasting the corrupt brilliance of Paganism with the austere and self-reliant teaching of early Christianity." One knows all this "business" by heart, the orgies, the arena, the Christian maiden with her hair let down her back, the Roman conversion in the nick of time, the glimpse of the "bloated and sensual figure of the emperor."

Feasts and Catacombs

It all lies outside the pale of literature; it should be reserved for the Marie Corellis and the Wilson Barretts. That Sienkiewicz has taken up this facile theme and that (as I gather from epitomes of his plot) he has treated it in very much the old conventional way, lessens my respect for this talent.[16]

Gosse inadvertently contradicted himself by calling the theme of *Quo Vadis?* "facile," as in his own case the opposite was true if the very subject deterred him from reading the novel. To attract the general readership and to earn universal applause with such a theme was certainly not an easy task. Too many predecessors and contemporaries had to be obliterated. The key to the novelist's success lay in his artistry.

III *Plot and Structure*

Quo Vadis? begins with an episode which has appeared time and again in world literature. A young man returns to his senior relative after a prolonged absence. In a similar way, Turgenev began *A Nest of Gentlefolk* as did Dostoyevsky his *The Possessed.* Sienkiewicz himself had used the same device with some modifications in the opening of *The Polaniecki Family,* but it was ingeniously adjusted and applied in the novel of ancient Rome.

Vinitius is an officer returning from the Middle East, and his uncle Petronius, the former governor of Bithynia, is glad to hear, not so much of the nephew's military exploits, but of the country where he displayed considerable administrative talent. Vinitius is out of touch with life in Rome, so he listens with curiosity to local gossip, which presents the author with an excellent opportunity to supply much information in a natural and inconspicuous way. Petronius takes his habitual bath and hospitably invites his nephew to do the same. This provides the writer with an excuse to acquaint the reader with various arrangements in Roman houses, to describe the bath ritual, to display a great number of typical properties, and to introduce different kinds of servants and residents of the household. During the carefree conversation, the names Aulus Plautius and Pomponia Graecina are casually mentioned. Presently Vinitius tells of his amorous adventure. Thus, in addition to the affairs of the court another plot gets under way. Both men discuss the possible plan of action. The more experienced uncle does not want to act hastily and makes the decision to investigate the matter on the spot by visiting Aulus Plautius' home. As an exposition, the leisurely first chapter is a masterpiece of condensation and an excellent start.

For some time the author continues his narrative in the same spirit, revealing Roman customs and maintaining the reader's interest without the machinations of an adventurous plot. The sketch of a fish, drawn by Lygia on the sand, is just a fleeting detail. Petronius finds an ingenious way of securing Lygia for his nephew without the ceremony of marriage. As he wants to preserve appearances, Lygia must arrive first in the emperor's palace and be present at the banquet. This, of course, is an opportunity for describing the lavish life of Rome. The fate of Lygia seems to be sealed, as the efforts of Aulus Plautius to regain his ward are in vain.

However, the writer springs his first major surprise. Unknown culprits kidnap Lygia, and all endeavors to locate her fail. In his despair, Vinitius gladly accepts the services of Chilo. There is only one enigmatic clue—a fish drawn on the sand by Lygia. The cunning Greek starts inquiries which finally connect Lygia with the Christians. Now Vinitius, in turn, assumes the role of a kidnapper. The superhuman strength of Ursus frustrates the assault.

In the initial chapters *Quo Vadis?* gives the impression of its being a historical novel of manners. Gradually the elements of an adventurous tale and of a detective novel change the course of the narrative. The author weaves into the fabric of the story several kidnappings, escapes, and releases. He complicates the romance with a casual treason (the episode with Chrysothemis), and an interference of a dangerous rival, Poppea; he demonstrates the tracing of Lygia and the Christians by a clever sleuth. A brief idyllic episode precedes the two major disasters—the burning of Rome and the anti-Christian campaign. The roles are reshuffled: Chilo becomes a prosecutor of Christians, and the open hostility of Nero comes forward. Lygia, rescued from the conflagration, is imprisoned.

Some incidents of the novel are reminiscent of the *Trilogy.* Yet in *Quo Vadis?* there is less artistic justification for adventurous components. They are loosely blended with the main conflict between Christianity and paganism, and occasionally they appear too flimsy. What in the *Trilogy* seems a natural emanation of the chivalrous era, in *Quo Vadis?* looks like a stereotyped set of tricks. It is possibly this inconsistency which discouraged some sophisticated readers.

The happy finale comes as a surprise, but in fact it has been carefully prepared. Very early in the novel, Ursus distinguishes himself by his physical strength. The author points to his power by introducing an episode with the famous athlete Kroto, whom Ursus (meaning "bear" in Latin) overcomes without any difficulty. The news of this feat reaches Nero, who hears of Ursus once again immediately before the start of the anti-Christian campaign. The emperor remarks that a mortal who strangled Kroto deserves a statue in the Forum. A direct hint of the incident in the circus is enclosed in the admission of the giant clumsily trying to feed the injured Vinitius: "It is easier to drag a bison out of the recess of the forest." And when the amused patrician asks him whether he really took such beasts by the horns, Ursus replies that he was afraid of them before he was twenty years old but that later he performed the trick.

As the novelist avoided any precise dates, he was not hampered by chronology. This made some structural solutions relatively easier. Both Vinitius and Petronius, involved directly or indirectly in the love affair, were also Nero's courtiers; this linked the romantic plot with political implications. The drawing of a fish, at first resembling a childish reflex, anticipated the search of Chilo. His closer acquaintance with the Christians made him later useful to Tigellinus in diverting from Nero the responsibility for the burning of Rome.

The novel was divided into two parts. In the first part, more serene moods and individual affairs prevailed; in the second, a gloominess was brought on by an increase in horror and mass scenes. The ensuing contrast was a conscientious structural means of strengthening the effect of the finale.

Notwithstanding the meticulous planning of the plot, Sienkiewicz increased cohesion by using his well-tested devices of anticipation and flashbacks. Predictions appeared almost from the outset. In the first chapter, Petronius asked his nephew various, apparently irrelevant questions, whether he took part in the races; whether he wrote verses; whether he played the lute and sang; and from the negative replies, he deduced that the young warrior was in no danger from Nero. But he added slyly, "Thou art a comely young man; hence Poppea may fall in love with thee. But no, she is too experienced. . ."[17] These casual words found a sinister echo at first in Chapter 31, where in spite of her experience Poppea, angered by the affair of Nero with the Vestal Rubria, sought oblivion with Vinitius. That was, however, only the beginning of the complications. The vanity of Poppea was hurt, and she did her utmost to harm Lygia and Vinitius; she was present at the meeting where the future extermination of the Christians was discussed. A small nucleus grew to surprising dimensions.

The attitude of Petronius toward Nero anticipated his imminent clash with the ruler. After the death of his child, Nero raised a lament and accused Petronius of being responsible for her death. The *arbiter elegantiae* seized a silk kerchief which Nero wore on his neck, put it in his mouth, and said with sad gravity: "Sire, burn Rome and the world from grief but save for us Thy voice!" In this particular moment he risked everything—and won; but it was all too clear that such victories could not continue forever. Although he enjoyed the favor of Nero, he was aware of the precariousness of his position. When the ruler invited him and Vinitius for a trip to Antium, he remarked: "Were I not among those invited, it would mean that I must die; I do not expect that to happen before the journey to Achaia . . ."[18]

At last the inevitable happened. Petronius' intervention on behalf of the Christians failed. For some time Nero still played the role of a forgiving and generous monarch. He declared that Petronius was his companion and friend, and so should expect only forgiveness. After this magnanimous statement a thought flashed through Petronius' mind: "I lost and I perished"; and indeed his peril was only a matter of time. The reader was allowed to participate in his sublime game and to experience all its hazardous thrills.

Petronius' appeal to Nero—that he should burn Rome rather than lose his voice—was ominous. Ironically, from the mouth of the *arbiter elegantiae* came the first mention of the burning of the Roman capital. This theme returned in the conversations of Nero with his courtiers. The emperor complained that boredom tortured him and that he could not stand the sight of Rome, with its collapsing houses and filthy lanes. Then Tigellinus asked him: "Caesar, thou sayest, 'if some angry god would destroy the city . . . art thou not a god'?"[19] On the eve of the holocaust, Lygia interrupted her prayer, saying that the whole city seemed to be on fire; it was red from the sunset. "And indeed the sun set strangely. Its huge shield descended by half behind the Janicula hills and the sky was filled with a red gleam. Lygia repeated her remark of Rome and Peter added: The wrath of God is resting upon it!"[20]

The romance of Vinitius was foretold in his account of the night spent in the temple of Mopsus. In a dream the youth saw a god predicting a great change in his life through love. As to Vinitius' safety, the apostle Peter assured him that he would not suffer any harm from Nero. When Petronius warned his nephew to beware of Poppea's revenge, Vinitius replied:

"I will not! Not a single hair will fall off my head." "If you think that you have surprised me once again," remarked Petronius, "you are mistaken; but how did you get this certainty?"

"The apostle Peter told me."

Now Petronius realized the power of the young man's faith; but he still advised him to take some precautionary steps to insure that Peter's forecast would not fail. The time would come when hope seemed absurd. Yet the patrician still repeated to Lygia that the Apostle told him to trust in God.[21]

The sudden career of Chilo was also discreetly foreshadowed. When Vinitius, angered by his denunciation of Lygia, flogged him, Petronius did not approve of the punishment and said: "As to Chilo, I should have given him five pieces of gold; but as it was thy will to flog him, it was better to flog him to death, for who knows but in time senators will bow to him, as today they are bowing to our cobbler-knight, Vatinius."[22] Naturally Petronius, who was not a visionary, relied on his knowledge of the world and human nature, while the Christian clairvoyance was irrational. In this way, the same structural device marked a dividing line between the two philosophies.

In view of the relatively compact structure of the novel, flashbacks were of less importance. Nonetheless, they occasionally played a useful role. Full structural use was made of the symbolic fish drawn by Lygia. The mishap of Vinitius during his attempt to kidnap Lygia reappeared in different disguises. At first, the author simply gave a dramatic report of the event which took place before the eyes of the readers. Second, the eyewitness Chilo revived the scene in his memory and began to fear that he would be responsible for it. Third, the Greek received from Vinitius another description of the accident. Realizing that it was a result of some agreement between Vinitius and the Christians, Chilo not only accepted the suggestion but enriched the story with his own embellishments. Fourth, the episode found some repercussions in Petronius' letter to his nephew, with special stress put on the strength of Ursus. Fifth, a distorted version was rendered to Nero. And here again Ursus was the main hero, so that Tigellinus vowed to find him. At last, the story was retold to Nero by Chilo. On this occasion the report acquired a sinister coloring, as the Greek accused Vinitius of deceiving the emperor. The motif was treated as a musical theme and produced different emotions.

Another repetitive incident was the attempted murder of Glaucos by Chilo. It was inserted in order to complicate the search for Lygia. At first Chilo presented his own account to Vinitius, completely distorting the truth. Later a new portrait of Glaucos was drawn in Chapter 23 when the physician took care of the wounded Vinitius. Then the full truth was unveiled when Glaucos recognized Chilo who was summoned by Vinitius. But the final echo of the episode sounded in the hour of martyrdom. Glaucos looked down from the cross at his executioner who betrayed him, deprived him of his wife and children, set upon him a killer and when all this was forgiven in the name of Christ, once again handed his victim over into the hands of hangmen.[23] Now Chilo broke down, asked forgiveness and received it. From that moment, he became a different man, worthy of baptism.

The composition of the novel owes its monumental outline to the distinct prominence of a few collective scenes devised on a grandiose scale. There are only four of them, distributed in the narrative with majestic symmetry: Caesar's banquet, the gathering of the Christians in the catacombs, the holocaust in Rome, and the triple martyrdom of Christians. Around these basic components, the author arranged the other episodes.

In his review of the novel *Sur la pierre blanche* by Anatole France, Sienkiewicz made some remarks which clarified the principles of his own technique. He praised the French writer for attributing to his characters the ideas expected from them, and expressing these ideas in an appropriate style. In this way, France created an artistic illusion full of charm, especially for the "so-called cultured people."[24] This was just the kind of illusion that the Polish novelist sought to achieve in his own works.

Dialectically the characters Petronius and Chilo are given prominence. Their display of wit is dazzling and their intellectual juggling in the discussions breathtaking. Petronius specializes in satirical sallies. In the verbal duels in which he mercilessly crushes his opponents his method is not unlike the dialogues of Plato. Chilo excels in repartees comparable to the *logomachias* in the ancient dramas. He does not necessarily use the noblest kind of weapons, and sometimes his verbal fencing turns into vituperation; but in such kind of contest he is impressive.

Nero's speech was a faithful mirror of his twisted personality. A typical conversation took place after the burning of Rome. Tigellinus warned him that one of the descendants of Augustus might proclaim himself Caesar. Nero coolly responded that in the meantime he would ascertain that there were no such descendants. To Tigellinus' remark that the crowd desired revenge, the ruler raised his hand and recited a versified epigram which he had just composed. Then he sought a suitable victim among

his courtiers whose death would pacify the mob. After two un-
acceptable suggestions, he bluntly told Tigellinus that it was he
who had burned Rome. The face of the prefect of the pretorians
shrunk like the muzzle of a dog ready to bite, and he told the
emperor that he only obeyed the order he had received. An exchange of jokes suddenly turned into a struggle for survival:

> "Tigellinus," said Nero, "dost thou love me?"
> "Thou knowest, Sire."
> "Sacrifice thyself for me."
> "Oh divine Caesar," answered Tigellinus, "Why present the sweet
> drink which I may not raise to my lips? The people are muttering and
> rising. Dost thou wish the pretorians also to rise?"[25]

Such dynamic exchanges of verbal thrusts appeared in *Quo
Vadis?* whenever the situation required them. Despite the
archaic background and the efforts to faithfully convey the
atmosphere of the ancient world, the diction was elastic, adapted
not only to individual tempers and intellects, but to the fluctuat-
ing moods. As was habitual among Latin writers, the author
occasionally mixed direct and indirect speech. This was helpful
in blending the conversations into the texture of the work. The
purposeful distribution of dialogues helped avoid lengthy descriptive passages, animated the story, and created an impression
of calm, balanced harmony, coordinated with the rhythm of
incidents.

The language of *Quo Vadis?* conveyed a sense of the epoch and
at the same time excelled in clarity and polish. Latinisms now
played quite a different role than in the *Trilogy*. They were used
chiefly in naming the objects and properties of the setting. Sienkiewicz did not flaunt erudition but used these Latinisms deftly.
J. Kaden Bandrowski, a writer belonging to a different literary
school, grasped the singular fascination of Sienkiewicz's diction:

> I think that as far as some classicism or order in the structure of clauses
> and sentences is concerned, Sienkiewicz will prove to be more correct
> and permanent (i.e., than Zeromski). I believe that if someone who
> even did not know our language listens to his prose, on the basis of
> the balanced structure of clauses and the measure which distinguishes
> even his longest periods, and on the basis of the harmony of words with

the tempo of syntactic structures, he would compare the texture of this prose to classic musical compositions. Note that in his prose this master never loses hold of the correctness of syntax, never sacrifices the ideal perfection to the ecstasies of fleeting moments.[26]

The mastery of style in *Quo Vadis?* did not depend on obtrusive mannerisms. The novelist did not try to imitate Latin syntactic patterns as did Kraszewski in *Nero's Rome*. He did not intentionally put the verbs at the end of the clauses as he sometimes did in the *Trilogy*. The classic aspect of his style was due to the balance of the resources of his native tongue. These were the qualities of *Quo Vadis?* which impressed once more its American translator Jeremiah Curtin.[27]

The initial triumph of the novel was so dramatic that it astonished editors and booksellers. "What makes the book popular?" asked a publisher in *Book News:* "What makes a book sell? Can *Quo Vadis?* be an accepted standard, and if so, when will it be repeated? For that book leads or stands high in four of the five lists. . . . And these relative scales are of the work in the regular and fine cloth bindings. The paper-covered reprints and editions have sold thousands strong but do not count in the comparison here."[28] As late as 1937, the French Larousse Encyclopedia affirmed this statement: "This was one of the most extraordinary successes registered in the history of the book."[29] As a novelistic vision of ancient Rome and early Christianity, *Quo Vadis?* has not yet been surpassed and in this respect its longevity was remarkable.

The repercussions of this novel in music, the theater, films, the arts, and even everyday life were impressive. In various countries it was appreciated for its educational value. It has been included in the books recommended for American colleges.[30] It still belongs among those publications reprinted and regularly purchased by public libraries. Abridged versions for youth are available in many languages—Dutch, German, Italian, French, English, and others. In Italy, after censoring some passages describing the banquet in Nero's palace, the Church introduced it into seminaries. The Swiss Radio-Beromunster organized a series of broadcasts for youth in 1957, based on *Quo Vadis?*.[31] The last

American edition of the novel was published in 1961 with new illustrations.

The narrative which captivated Sienkiewicz's contemporaries found an impressive echo in an early American review by Nathan Haskell Dole:

It is said that if a person standing at the foot of Niagara merely touches the awful sheet of water with a finger, he is drawn irresistibly in; and so if a person begins this book, the torrential sweep of its immensity becomes instantly absorbing. It is one of the great books of our day.[32]

CHAPTER 7

Birth of a Commonwealth

I Struggle for Survival

T HE first signals referring directly to Sienkiewicz's novel on medieval Poland appeared in 1891. The following year, he discussed some aspects of the forthcoming work, but other obligations still absorbed him. A decision to concentrate on the new project was taken toward the close of 1895. At that time the novelist had accumulated a considerable quantity of research material. Actual writing began in 1896 and was accompanied by further preparatory studies. The writing of the novel lasted over four years. Total work including introductory studies took almost ten years.

Information on Polish life in the Middle Ages was sparse. Sienkiewicz himself wondered why the reign of Nero left such an abundance of historical data that the main problem was one of proper selection, while the relatively recent period of Polish history remained so obscure. "We know perfectly well," he stated, "what a Roman of the first century A.D. thought and felt; but what did a Pole or a Lithuanian think during the reign of Prince Witold, this is a problem arousing thousands of doubts."[1]

Sienkiewicz was not discouraged, and with his customary conscientiousness he made every effort to become familiar with the available sources. The list of books which he consulted was quite impressive.[2] Not only did he peruse the works of modern historians but also the old chronicles, documents, and letters written in Polish and other languages. The author was indebted to the outstanding fifteenth-century chronicler Jan Dlugosz and to a study entitled *Jadwiga and Jagiello* by Karol Szajnocha. Other works and materials supplied many minor but valuable details which helped to reconstitute the historical events as well as the course of daily life. The novelist intended to make a trip to Gdansk and Malbork in order to visit the relics of the Teutonic Order; in September 1899, he visited the battlefield at Tannenberg, which he described in the epilogue of the novel.

A close historical examination of *The Teutonic Knights* is flattering to the author but reveals some inconsistencies. For instance, Sienkiewicz intimated that the Teutonic Order treated Queen Jadwiga, daughter of the Hungarian King Louis, with particular respect. A modern historian would reject this surmise. In the novel, Jadwiga is a pious woman living an ascetic kind of life and always dons the black robe of a nun. Recently it was shown that the Queen did not shun the entertainments of the Royal Court. As to Jagiello, the Lithuanian Prince elected to the throne of the Commonwealth, he was neither an uneducated primitive nor a person lacking common sense but a man quite fit for his royal duties. Sienkiewicz seemed to value the monarch highly; moreover, being aware that Dlugosz was ill-disposed toward Jagiello he omitted a few details which could disparage the image of the King, e.g., superstitious mood, fear of witchcraft, and so forth.

Sienkiewicz was not concerned about the minute accuracy of the historical background; instead, he attached much importance to typical data illustrating the fundamental tendencies of the period. He did not abuse the privileges customarily granted to writers of historical fiction but did not hesitate to take advantage of them when this suited his artistic design. His intuition occasionally helped him guess the incidents still unknown by his contemporaries, e.g., in the Battle of Grunwald he introduced units of peasant infantry.

Besides the fictional characters, a few historical figures appeared in the novel, but their role was different than in previous works. They did not interfere directly in the romantic developments. A planned execution of Zbyszko was canceled not because of the grace of the king but because of an ingenious intervention by Danusia. On the other hand, the fictional characters did not produce any immediate impact on state affairs, as happened sometimes in the *Trilogy*.

[*148*]

Describing historical personages in *The Teutonic Knights*, the author followed the historians; but he selected and arranged the features in such a way that they appeared as individual portraits, originally designed. This applied to Jadwiga and Jagiello, as well as to Witold, whose image lacked some of the splendor conveyed by history. Sometimes the author quoted the texts of his sources. The independent treatment of history and fiction gave him more freedom of action in manipulating the incidents of the plot.

As a vision of the past, *The Teutonic Knights* surpassed the earlier works by its versatility. Political conflicts and military clashes did not overshadow the author's picture of the era. Now he was more than ever aware that the fabric of national life was complex. Sienkiewicz showed different trends, tendencies, passions, and aspirations. He introduced not only various categories of squires, the king and his court, but also knights of native and foreign origin, soldiers, burghers, pedlars, clergymen, monks, farmers, knaves, and peasants. Scholars did not appear in any more significant role. The University of Cracow had been established in 1364, but at the end of the fourteenth century it was in a state of decline. Only after a generous donation bequeathed by Queen Jadwiga was it reorganized in 1400, and it subsequently attained international prominence. Yet mention of the University occurred in the text, which proved that its significance was not overlooked.

As in Sienkiewicz's other historical novels, there is in *The Teutonic Knights* a romantic plot parallel to historical incidents. As in *Pan Michael*, two girls are involved. Zbyszko of Bogdaniec fell in love with Danusia, and for a long time he saw Jagienka, a favorite of his uncle Macko, only as a good friend. Almost until the end of the novel the situation remained unchanged, even after Danusia died. The final stage of this entanglement was, of course, the same as in *Pan Michael*—Zbyszko married Jagienka.

The motif of Danusia is cleverly interwoven with the other elements of the novel. Her misfortunes were not a result of romantic complications but of a political feud. As the daughter of a Polish squire, Jurand, owner of an estate at the frontier between Poland and the Teutonic Order, this twelve-year-old girl became a pawn in the intrigues of the Knights who conspired to make Jurand harmless to the interests of the Order.

Pursuing the policy of aggression, the knights exploited every chance to harass their Polish neighbors. In spite of the peace treaty between the two countries, they assaulted a local Polish prince and took him prisoner. They released him only at the intervention of King Jagiello. During this incident Jurand's beloved wife died. Since that time, his only thought was revenge, and he relentlessly annoyed the Order. The squire made his estate a stronghold and kept the captured Teutonic prisoners in the cellar. The Knights were unable to overcome him in direct combat, so they conceived a diabolic plan which they ruthlessly executed. Aware of how deeply Jurand was attached to his only daughter, they kidnapped her in order to blackmail the father.

Prior to his wife's death, Jurand treated the Knights in a neighborly way; then revenge overpowered his humane feelings. Nevertheless, he fought against the Order in an open, straightforward manner. When he learned of the kidnapping of his daughter, the voice of love prevailed in his soul and, in order to regain his child, he was ready and willing to meet all conditions set by his foes. He trusted his enemies and believed that they acted in good faith. Danusia's singing, which he heard at night, assured him that she was alive. When instead of his daughter, the knights showed him another girl, supposedly the only one whom they held prisoner, his patience snapped. He furiously attacked his gloating tormentors and slaughtered many of them before he was overpowered. Siegfried, the superior of the Knights, had promised to release him. As a chivalrous man, he kept his word; but he ordered the hangman to burn out Jurand's only eye, to sever his right hand, and to tear out his tongue. Only an accident saved the victim from death.

Although cruelly maimed, Jurand learned to communicate with other people. The squire became a completely transformed man. Instead of hardening his heart, his agony taught him forgiveness and love. Siegfried, his arch-enemy and executioner, was captured by the Poles and brought to Jurand's estate to be punished. Jurand took a knife and cut the prisoner's bonds, thus denouncing hatred and wrath; he died like a saint. In this manner Sienkiewicz completed the chain of moral reflections which he inaugurated in *The Trilogy* and continued in *Quo Vadis?*.

The behavior of the Teutonic Knights was invariably in direct contrast to the sublime gospel symbolized by the squire Jurand at the end of his life. The Order cruelly oppressed the native Prussian and Lithuanian tribes under the pretext of conversion and waged continuous wars against their neighbors. It pretended to practice humility, but it displayed monstrous conceit; it proclaimed piety, but its hyprocisy was revolting. Zbyszko, a reckless youth, assaulted through sheer ignorance a Teutonic envoy, Kuno Liechtenstein, and although the envoy was unharmed, capital punishment awaited the assailant. When some Poles requested Kuno to intervene on behalf of the youth, the envoy declared that as a humble monk he bore no grudge, but as a representative of the majesty of the Order, he could not forgive the offense.

Lies, deceit, hypocrisy, treachery, perjury, blackmail—these were the methods employed by the Order against their opponents. Whenever they committed a crime, they played the role of injured victims. They indulged in debauchery and behaved with extreme cruelty. In vain the superiors of the Order, such as Konrad von Jungingen, condemned the corruption creeping among the knightly brothers. Newcomers from the more distant foreign lands joined the Order in good faith. For this reason they found themselves in conflict with other knights; one of them, having learned of the kidnapping of Jurand's daughter, raised a voice of protest and presently fell a victim of murder. De Lorche, another foreign volunteer, abandoned the Knights and joined the Poles.

The Order applied a policy of exploitation of its subjects. The arbitrary taxes imposed on the population spread misery and poverty, so that complaints in their domains were universally heard. The knights disobeyed the warnings issued by their grand master. Decent individuals were helpless, as the whole policy of the Order relied on injustice. No wonder that the prophecy of Ste. Brigit included a prediction of disaster. People prayed for a day of reckoning which would put an end to this nest of evil.

Sienkiewicz's description of the Teutonic Order and its policy depended on selected historical sources. On the other hand, the writer bore in mind that the Order was the nucleus of future Prussian power. During the Reformation, one of the grand masters secularized the Order and transformed it into a Duchy paying homage to the Polish kings. Gradually the state emancipated itself, gained strength, and became one of the great military powers of Central Europe. It was mainly responsible for the partitions of Poland.

Sienkiewicz attributed to the modern Prussian Kingdom the same brutal aggressiveness which he had noticed in the Teutonic Order. The spirit remained unchanged; only the methods were modified. The Prussian administration used power and cunning to expropriate the native Poles and to replace them by German settlers. It introduced a program of *Kulturkampf* aimed at the complete Germanization of the Polish territories. It repressed protests by violence, which did not spare even children. These incidents added special poignancy to the narrative of the medieval predecessors of the Prussian Kingdom.

II *Seeds of Growth*

Besides his aim to clarify the Prussian dilemma, there was an additional reason why after the *Trilogy* Sienkiewicz turned to Polish medieval history. This was the period when the foundations of national life were established. The vast territory of the Commonwealth was as yet sparsely populated; the large forests full of wild beasts challenged the settlers. This situation offered unlimited possibilities to people with courage, initiative, and vigor. From this point of view, the conditions were not unlike those of the American pioneers. The value of manpower was high. One of the ambitions nurtured by the squires was to have many children, thereby insuring the expansion and continuity of their achievements.

Macko of Bogdaniec was a worthy exponent of these aspirations. He had reasons for hating the Teutonic Knights. He felt bitter toward Kuno von Liechtenstein who scornfully rejected his plea on behalf of his nephew. An arrow shot from an ambush incapacitated him for months. Nevertheless, for Macko war was mainly a chance to grow rich in order to buy land.

Macko's main ambition was to promote his clan and to secure its prosperity. That is why he cared more about his nephew than about himself. He observed knightly dignity and honor, but this did not hinder him in acting with sly shrewdness. Although he had no special education, he displayed much wit in a medieval fashion. When he had to leave his estate, he realized that it was exposed to the attacks of his unfriendly neighbors. He visited one of them, named Wilk, with whom he had a long controversy concerning property. He started by declaring that he wished to yield a controversial piece of land. The hot-tempered Wilk was taken by surprise; he did not want to appear less generous and in turn pleaded with Macko to take over the land which the cunning old man humbly accepted. When the matter was settled, Macko indulged in a typical monologue: "Lord Jesus is all-powerful, there is no doubt of that; but there are also ways and means to win heavenly grace, and man must be prudent."[3] Here Macko looked like a worthy ancestor of Zagloba with one difference—he applied his wit to practical purposes and not to adventurous fancies.

Representing the young generation, Zbyszko exhibited more sublime qualities. He was an enthusiastic follower of the noble principles of knighthood and eagerly sought an opportunity to earn distinction. He gave as well the impression of a boy whose naïve ebullience deserved indulgence. Pain and grief hastened his maturity. He was quite a different man when he challenged the Teutonic knight Rotgier to a deadly duel and when he joined a Lithuanian prince in order to seek vengeance. Until the end, however, he maintained a degree of naïveté, which added charm to his romance with Jagienka.

In Sienkiewicz's earlier historical novels some protagonists experienced a spiritual transformation; this happened to Kmicic, Chilo Chilonides in the final hours of his life, and partly to Zagloba. But the changes were either not systematically observed, or else they did not go too deep, so that the essential traits of the person concerned remained. In *The Teutonic Knights* the psychological growth of several characters, especially Jurand and Zbyszko was much more pronounced.

A considerable number of secondary characters was portrayed with Sienkiewicz's usual skill. They did not imprint themselves in the minds of readers with the same clear-cut distinction as the figures of the *Trilogy*. Yet they conveyed the impression of people belonging to the period concerned and gave a fair idea of the author's concept of medieval Poland. Among them the abbot stood supreme. He was an amusing mixture of a churchman and a knight, capable of wilful despotism and furious outbursts of anger, as well as of cordial kindness. The itinerant merchant specializing in selling the fantastic sacred relics and Zbyszko's devoted Czech servant Hlava were valuable additions to the novelist's gallery of portraits.

Sienkiewicz often turned specimens of unique physical power into simple characters. Such was Roch Kowalski in *The Deluge*, whom Zagloba succeeded in persuading that he was his uncle; the brothers Kiemlicz, depending blindly on their father: Longinus in *With Fire and Sword*; and Ursus in *Quo Vadis?*. In *The Teutonic Knights* the two provincial churls, Wilk and Cztan, also lacked wit; but in most cases extraordinary strength did not involve any intellectual handicap. One of the prominent courtiers at the king's castle twisted an iron chopper with his bare fingers as if it were made of cardboard. Another at a tournament in Torun felled twelve Teutonic knights "with great glory to himself and to his nation." Other feats were even more astonishing. As a matter of fact, the autor intimated that in this respect the Poles were at that time superior to Westerners. They owed their vigor not only to innate qualities but to simpler and healthier living:

The knights of Western Europe were in those days accustomed to luxury and comfort, while the squires in Great and Little Poland, as well as in Mazovia, were austere and self-denying. Because of this they even aroused the admiration of enemies and strangers by their strength of body and endurance.[4]

Women were not much inferior to men. Jagienka helped her future husband kill a bear, and she used to crush nuts simply by sitting on them. Perhaps it was not a coincidence that Sienkiewicz pointedly named western Poland and Mazovia as the reservoir of strong men. In the *Trilogy* the warriors were recruited from the eastern regions of the Commonwealth, and the strongest was the unbeatable Longinus, a Lithuanian. In *The Teutonic Knights* the Poles were portrayed as a young, healthy, and robust nation.

Valor was one of the features which could be expected from such a dynamic society. However, the author did not identify it with aggressiveness. The only purpose of the Polish knights was to defend their native land. If they struggled with the Teutonic Order, they were compelled to this by intolerable provocations, assaults, and threats. Following the ideals of knighthood, they preserved the rules of fair play and did not adopt the methods of their foes. They loathed treason and base frauds.

The pathetic mood of the novel was centered around Jurand, a monumental expression of paternal woe. Danusia provoked a moving effect. The turmoil of history involved this tender, charming maiden in a test for which she was utterly unprepared and which crushed her body and mind. Her lamentable singing in a Teutonic tower, heard by her father, was irresistibly touching. Horror accompanied many episodes and reached its peak when Siegfried saw the corpse of Rotgier terribly mutilated by Zbyszko and directed the executioner to maim Jurand. The German's suicide resulted from the moral shock of the unexpected foregiveness granted by his victim. The ensuing mental collapse was translated into the language of a vision reminiscent of the macabre fantasies of some symbolist artists.

The Battle of Grunwald, in which the Teutonic Knights suffered a decisive defeat, was added as an illustration of the historical verdict. Here, as in the finale of *With Fire and Sword,* the author let history speak, adopting the attitude of a chronicler; in this manner the epilogue acquired weightier significance. Structurally, this episode was only loosely connected with the novel, although many leading characters took part in the event. The battle occurred ten years after the plot had run its course.

In *The Teutonic Knights* Sienkiewicz made an attempt to create his own version of archaic Polish. He inserted in his diction some elements from ancient literary monuments and the dialect of the Polish highlanders who preserved many old forms and expressions. The experiment was successful and harmonized well with the content.

The critics welcomed the novel with respect and valued it highly, but for a long time they favored the *Trilogy*. Its reception aboard was cooler. In America, publishers, encouraged by the successes of the previous novels, expected it to become another best seller. Four different translators simultaneously began to render it into English. Parts of the novel were published before the whole text was available. For various reasons the reaction of the readers was disappointing.

The Second World War put *The Teutonic Knights* in a different perspective. Now the episodes which for many years seemed exaggerated or just melodramatic appeared almost clairvoyant. Antoni Golubiew, a contemporary Polish author of historical novels, frankly admitted in an essay that "The war 'revealed' for us *The Teutonic Knights* to a great extent."[5] In England Lord Vansittart wrote an introduction to a new translation of the novel published in 1943.

In more recent times Sienkiewicz's medieval novel has been sometimes considered superior to his other writings. According to Alina Nofer,

The Teutonic Knights infinitely surpasses the *Trilogy* by the truth of life and the vision of its real conflicts and beauty. . . . From the historical material the brilliant imagination of the artist succeeded in creating a work equalled only by a few novels in Polish literature. This really magnificent monument of 'fame and glory' of the nation became almost a monument of Sienkiewicz's 'fame and glory.'[6]

However, it is doubtful whether the medieval novel, in spite of its unquestionable qualities, can ever overshadow the earlier works. It lacks their monolithic impetus, restful vigor and fighting swing.

CHAPTER 8

Youth and Adventure

I A Prelude to Glory

WHEN Sienkiewicz announced his intention to write a new novel linked with the history of King Jan Sobieski, his admirers expected that its content would include the victory at Vienna over the Turks. *On the Field of Glory* did not fulfill this hope. The title was misleading, as the narrative did not contain any outstanding historical events. Preparations for a war with the infidels were in full swing, but the only armed clashes described by the author were duels among the gentry and a skirmish with brigands. To compensate for these shortcomings, the finale brought a review of the armed forces leaving for Vienna. The author planned a continuation which never materialized.

The contracts for this new novel were signed as early as November 1901. Two years later the beginning was written, and the end was ready in August 1905. Evidently the tempo of work was slow, as the novel was relatively short. The author serialized it in the weekly *Biesiada literacka*. Since the editors advertised the novel prematurely, the readers grew impatient. The writer published a letter asking his admirers for more patience. According-ing to Curtin, one of the main reasons for all these delays was the author's preoccupation with the Russo-Japanese War, which stirred the whole Polish community.

The action of *On the Field of Glory* took place during the winter of 1682–83, and as in other novels the opening was excellent. A group of travelers attacked by a pack of wolves was in serious trouble. The sudden arrival of a number of riders rescued them from danger. The nobleman Pagowski, traveling with his beautiful ward Sieninska, had to accept the hospitality of the squires to whom he owed his lucky escape. Several gentlemen bought the favor of the young lady, and one of them, Jacek Taczewski, challenged five of them to a duel and beat them all.

The basic plot was the rivalry of various suitors for the hand of the girl. One of them, her guardian, died from a stroke at the banquet given on the occasion of the betrothal. Another one was a rough, repulsive character who was capable of beating a woman. Finally, the poor, but noble Taczewski won and happily married Miss Sieninska. Immediately after the wedding he left with Sobieski for the Vienna expedition.

The narrative included episodes similar to these in other historical novels by Sienkiewicz: duels, assaults, kidnappings, and escapes. All of them were shown against the backdrop of everyday life. There was no intention to emphasize heroics, and the author treated some incidents in an almost satirical way. As to Taczewski, a poor but proud squire making a career by gallantry, he reminded the reader of his French predecessor in *The Three Musketeers*.

The characters were drawn with a practiced hand, but they lacked individual distinctiveness. In the narrative there was no evidence of the indirect pressure of more recent problems. *On the Field of Glory,* had little in common with the dilemmas of Sienkiewicz's generation.

Curtin wrote in his memoirs that only one person wrote to him about this novel, President Theodore Roosevelt. "He was immensely pleased with the book but knowing history as well, he wanted a battle." The translator himself admitted that nothing more vexatious had happened to him for years than the abruptness of this narrative.[1]

II *A Tale for Children*

Sienkiewicz was a devoted father. His children were his main concern during his lifetime. Every illness of his little Jadzia or Henio worried him. He felt very proud when his son became an outstanding high school pupil. His letters to intimate friends often included details regarding his son and daughter.

Children and adolescents appeared not only in the writer's short stories but also in his novels. Sometimes he attributed heroic features to them. In the tale "From the Memoirs of a Poznan Tutor" Michas made superhuman efforts to spare his mother any trouble. Orso bravely defended his little companion and took care of her. In *With Fire and Sword* a youth shot a dying Cossack in order to save him from further torture; he knew that he risked his life and when asked why he violated military discipline, he replied that he could not look at suffering. In *The Polaniecki Family* Litka sacrificed her secret love for the happiness of Polaniecki.

When Sienkiewicz conceived *In Desert and Wilderness*, his own children were already grown. However, his fondness for children had not subsided. He enjoyed the friendship of Wanda Ulanowska, the thirteen-year-old daughter of his friends in Cracow, and for quite a long time corresponded with her. In one of his letters he informed her of his new literary venture:

As in my opinion every novelist should write something for children at least once in his lifetime, I decided to begin and to finish next New Year's (1911) a novel bearing the title *Adventures of Two Children in Central Africa*. A Polish boy and an English girl will appear in it and beside them Bedouins, Arabs, and Negro cannibals, plus elephants, crocodiles, lions, hippopotami, etc. I wish to write it in such a way that not only children but thirteen-year old teen-agers and even grown-ups could read it with interest.[2]

Rudyard Kipling whose books found warm acclaim among the children all over the world could be one of Sienkiewicz's literary guides. The Polish author based his exotic novel on his own African experiences, which were still alive in his memory. Yet he did not rely exclusively in his reminiscences and completed them with additional studies and readings.

The novel resulted partly from educational considerations which caused increasing concern among the Polish people. The prolonged oppression in the German and Russian occupation produced harmful effects, and some vigorous counteraction seemed necessary. Sienkiewicz accepted the chairmanship of "Macierz" (Mother), a non-profit organization which took care of educational needs on a national scale. Such activity depended on funds which were difficult to obtain. Besides, even the best possible system of schooling depending on voluntary donations could not compare with regular educational systems of modern independent states. The failure of the revolutionary rising of 1905 created a depression which added to the problem.[3]

In their quest for educational influence, the Poles in the Austrian occupation established in 1910 the Boy Scout organization based on the example and instructions of General Baden-Powell and his English followers. Sienkiewicz's novel for children coincided with this movement, and he seemed to share some of its guiding ideals. There was no definite proof that the author was acquainted with it during his work on *In Desert and Wilderness,* but it was not improbable. Of course his previous writings anticipated many slogans and virtues which the Boy Scouts proclaimed, such as: patriotism, courage, physical and moral strength, common sense, and a spirit of leadership and companionship.

In his novel the writer combined various expedients enjoying perennial popularity among children. From the very outset he made it an adventure story developing such motifs as warfare, a treacherous kidnapping, a lucky escape, desperate predicaments, and successful rescues. The children in the book regained their freedom only to find themselves alone in the middle of the immense African continent; they were forced to rely on their own resources. Their sole companion was a Negro youth reminiscent of Friday in Defoe's novel, *Robinson Crusoe,* which was obviously the model of this part of the work. Finally, the author inserted his favorite romantic note, making a fragile, tiny, and sweet little girl a ward of the boy who eventually would become her husband.

In order to do justice to the novel, it should be compared with other works of the same genre published at the same time.[4] Before World War I many Polish books for children still followed the Positivist watchwords, which had already become obsolete in other spheres of life. A didactic and moralizing spirit prevailed. The main goal was to encourage humane feelings by showing instances of unselfish philanthropic attitudes and by encouraging individual self-reliance. The list of recommended qualities included chiefly diligence, thrift, devotion to family, especially to parents, and prudence. Such books were monotonous, colorless, and boring; they lacked imaginative swing and the element of adventure. Only a few authors, such as Konopnicka, Przyborowski and Uminski, departed from the generally adopted formula. Translations from other languages usually had little in common with specific Polish conditions and emotional needs.

Sienkiewicz kept his promise to Ulanowska. He treated his young readers in a serious way and even touched on some political problems. Naturally enough, such problems had to be simplified. Stas Tarkowski and Nelly Rawlison, whose fathers were employed in Africa, were kidnapped by the rebels of Mahdi and witnessed the war waged by him against the British administration. They became hostages through whom the rebels hoped to obtain the release of the wife and children of one of the insurgents. Sienkiewicz trusted the Englishmen as representatives of progress and did not indulge in any sallies against colonialism. On the other hand, he was fond of the Negroes and made Kali an attractive and reliable character.

Tarkowski impersonated skills and qualities which the author recommended to the younger generation. The boy's physique and stamina were impressive. He was a good swimmer, sharpshooter, and a fine horseman. He was capable of making hard decisions. At the same time, he was conscious of honor and dignity. He would never agree to abandon the faith of his fathers. The youth took care of Nelly with complete self-denial: for her he suffered humiliations and hunger; for her he begged and even stole; for her he saved the last drops of water when imminent death from thirst threatened. Naturally, such an accumulation of wonderful advantages and virtues was fantastic and even irritating. However, occasionally Tarkowski behaved like any normal boy revealing weakness and confusion. The author made his exploits tolerable by granting him help whenever the situation grew hopeless. Nelly was as charming as could be expected; she soon became aware of her influence and as a real little woman took advantage of it for the sake of those she loved.

[*161*]

Books for children change according to different tastes, educational trends, and fashions. *In Desert and Wilderness,* with its emphasis on the didactic message, may differ from books recommended for children in more recent time. One aspect of this novel remains unchallenged: the painting of African nature based on details of direct observation.

CHAPTER 9

Conclusion

THE international renown of Sienkiewicz among his contemporaries was not a stroke of luck but a well-earned success. In an unobtrusive way he met the longing for optimism felt not only in his own suppressed country but in other lands as well. His realism was genuine but polished and tame, so that it did not offend the conventionality of the age, and was acceptable to the expanding ranks of mass readers. The Polish background concurred with the widespread search for exotic values and anticipated the impending inclusion of the "marginal" nations in the mainstream of Western literature.

Sienkiewicz was an adroit exponent of the spirit of adventure which could not yet be satisfied by visual vehicles, still in *statu nascendi*. His portrayals lacked psychological perspicacity but were imaginative, consistent and memorable. His command of structural devices revealed the technical progress of traditional narrative skill. The superior qualities of his diction, enjoyed primarily by his own countrymen, partly survived in translations and contributed to the writer's universal appeal, especially as his English and French translators—at least a few of them—fulfilled their task with dedication.

Sienkiewicz's technical craft was noticeable in his minor works, but his main literary contribution belonged to the field of the historical narrative. The *Trilogy* conjured up the magic of seventeenth-century Poland, as colorful and thrilling as the American West; its special significance for the author's own countrymen can be readily understood. *Quo Vadis?* was acclaimed as the unrivaled vision of one of the most dramatic events of ancient times, and the seven decades of its renown showed that it could be easier bypassed than surpassed. *The Teutonic Knights* sounded

[*163*]

as an augury of an acute moral crisis which seemed exaggerated but was later confirmed. Technically, the alliance between a conscientious search for historical vision and the novel of adventure found in Sienkiewicz the most accomplished exponent.

The eclipse of the novelist's popularity coincided with World War I, which had a deep impact upon intellectual attitudes and literary tastes. The events did not confirm the rosy forecasts and dispelled the outdated optimistic reveries. Psychological interests turned to the subconscious sphere; a new concept of realism gained ground. Traditional literary criteria collapsed. In the new dynamic world, soft voices of the recent past were outshouted by the clamoring present. Technical media, preying mercilessly on Sienkiewicz and other writers, vulgarized some of his favorite devices and weakened their initial charm;[1] this was a part of the price which the novelist had to pay for his fame.

Even at the peak of his popularity, Sienkiewicz met with strong opposition. In france a campaign was started in order to safeguard French literature from the unwarranted invasion of foreigners. Léon Daudet wrote an essay criticizing *Quo Vadis?* as an example of undeserved success. But the cummulative effect of Sienkiewicz's craft, and his incomparable narrative zest were so infectious that they often overcame both esthetic reservations and conscious criticism. This curious process was recently demonstrated by Witold Gombrowicz, a tireless foe of obsolete myths and meaningless conventions:

I am reading Sienkiewicz. What tormenting reading. We say, "that is bad enough," and we continue to read. We exclaim, "an intolerable soap opera!" and we still read in enchantment. What a powerful genius!— and there never was such a first-rate writer of the second-rate class. This is a second-rate Homer, a first-rate Dumas, Senior. Sienkiewicz, this magician, this seducer, planted in our heads Kmicic and Wolodyjowski and the Great Hetman, and corked them up. . . . If the history of literature adopted as a criterion the influence of art on people, Sienkiewicz—this demon, this catastrophe of our mind, this wrecker should occupy in it five times more space than Mickiewicz. . . . His world is fierce, powerful, magnificent, has all the qualities of the real world but a label is stuck to it, "for entertainment," and for this reason he has an additional advantage—it does not terrify anyone.[2]

[*164*]

Conclusion

Sienkiewicz' place in the history of Polish literature is well determined. His international standing, though subject to obvious limitations, can hardly be ignored. He found the way to millions without debasing his literary craft or vocation. He did not discover any new vehicles of expression, but he combined skillfully the inherited ones and raised them to the level of virtuosity. He did not pave the way to the future but was a gifted exponent of the tendencies of his own period, which he reflected with dignity and dedication.

Occasionally Sienkiewicz still finds favorable response among major contemporary writers undaunted by transient fashions. Henri de Montherlant devoted to *Quo Vadis?* a carefully weighed eulogy.[3] In America Malcolm Cowley and William Faulkner paid a tribute to his *Trilogy*. Some recent trends in narrative prose restoring the role of incidents may favor better understanding of his writing proficiency. His universal appeal seems to last. In the years 1945–61 at least 303 volumes of the Polish novelist's works were reprinted in forty-three languages. This is assuredly evidence of his continuous living fascination among general readers.

Notes and References

Chapter One

1. This opinion was repeated in the essay on Sienkiewicz by Annie Russell Marble in *The Nobel Prize Winners* (New York, London, 1925), p. 226.

2. The detailed genealogy of the novelist is included in *Henryk Sienkiewicz, Kalendarz zycia i tworczosci*, by Julian Krzyzanowski (Warsaw, 1956, p. 23). This invaluable source of biographical data will henceforth be referred to as *Kalendarz*. Cf. also A. Bolescic-Kozlowski, *Henryk Sienkiewicz i rod jego* (Warsaw, 1917), p. 56, with a bibliography.

3. Adam Grzymala Siedlecki, author of a fine essay on Sienkiewicz based partly on his personal acquaintance with the writer, states that the Poles considered the Cieciszowski family as "three quarters of aristocracy." In *Niepospolici ludzie w dniu swoim powszednim* (Cracow, 1962), pp. 20–21.

4. Henryk Sienkiewicz, *Dziela, wyd. zbiorowe pod redakcja Juliana Krzyzanowskiego*, vol. XL, p. 129 (this collective edition of Sienkiewicz's works will be quoted as *Dziela*). Cf. also *Kalendarz*, pp. 25–26.

5. *Kalendarz*, p. 36 (after I. Chrzanowski). Some biographers assumed that Sienkiewicz could have taken part in the 1863 uprising. Krzyzanowski argues convincingly against this conjecture. Cf. his essay "Pȯwstanie styczniowe w tworczosci Sienkiewicza," *Dziedictwo literackie powstania styczniowego* (Warsaw, 1964), pp. 254–56.

6. The realistic aspect of *In Vain* was rather underestimated in *Henryk Sienkiewicz*, by Alina Nofer (Warsaw, 1959), pp. 33–35. This problem was clarified in *Pisarstwo Henryka Sienkiewicza*, by Andrzej Stawar (Warsaw, 1960), pp. 9–10.

7. An expressive silhouette of Sienkiewicz as a starting *littérateur* can be found in *Pani Helena*, by Tymon Terlecki (London, 1962), p. 115.

8. *Memories and Impressions of Helena Modjeska; an Autobiography* (New York, 1910), pp. 222–223.

9. *Ibid.*, pp. 242–44.

10. A. Stawar (*op. cit.*, pp. 217–19) disagrees with Julian Krzyzanowski, who rejected the gossip regarding Modjeska and Sienkiewicz. In Stawar's opinion, during his stay in America the writer behaved like a typical bohemian of the Przybyszewski period. Stanislaw Mackiewicz

expressed a similar view. On the other hand, T. Terlecki shared Krzy-zanowski's opinion (*op. cit.*, pp. 126–27).

11. Modjeska, *op. cit.*, p. 249.

12. *Ibid.*, p. 250.

13. *Kalendarz*, pp. 45–47.

14. From the letter to E. Lubowski, written in November 1876, *Dziela*, vol. LV, p. 435.

15. From a letter to Stefania Leo, *Dziela*, vol. LV, p. 429.

16. Quoted after *Kalendarz*, p. 57.

17. Letter to J. Horain, *Dziela*, vol. LV, pp. 240–41.

18. Cf. Zdzislaw Najder, "O 'Listach z podrozy' do Ameryki Henryka Sienkiewicza," *Pamietnik Literacki*, vol. XLVI:1, 1955, p. 84.

19. The essay was retranslated into Polish and printed in *Wiadomosci* (London) with comments by Jacek Bukowiecki, January 24, 1965, no. 4 (982).

20. *Kalendarz*, pp. 69–71.

21. Boleslaw Prus devoted to this episode of Sienkiewicz's career an amusing *feuilleton* on February 21, 1880, adding the subtitle, "What Sienkiewicz Does with the Fairer Half of Warsaw." In *Kroniki* (Warsaw, 1955), vol. IV, pp. 263–66.

22. Sienkiewicz made it clear that the daily edited by him would not become either bigoted or aristocratic. Cf. *Kalendarz*, pp. 99–100, and the introductory remarks on p. 9.

23. Letter to F. Smolka, *Dziela,* vol. LVI, p. 135.

24. The story was translated by W. R. Thompson, *The Catholic World*, vol. IV (1884), pp. 406–19.

25. Cf. Adam Grzymala Siedlecki, *op. cit.*, pp. 30–32. See also *Kalendarz*, pp. 153–55.

26. *Kalendarz*, p. 164.

27. The story of this marriage was shown in a humorous light by Tadeusz Boy-Zelenski, who was present at the wedding and knew various rumors circulating in society. In *Znasz li ten kraj?*, collective ed. of works, Warsaw s. a., vol. II, pp. 58–69. Adam Grzymala Siedlecki (*op. cit.*, p. 27) contended that nobody knew the real causes of the conflict.

28. Joseph Schafer, the editor of the memoirs of Jeremiah Curtin, stated that the publication of *Quo Vadis?* was a money maker: "It doubtless provided the means for the world tour the Curtins indulged in at the turn of the century and it also gave Mrs. Curtin a large share of her income for some years after Jeremiah's death." *Memoirs of Jeremiah Curtin* (Madison, 1940), p. 27. It should be added that the *Trilogy* was also a major success. *With Fire and Sword* appeared at the beginning of 1891, and the 1896 edition reprinted by Little, Brown & Co. was marked as "seventh."

Notes and References

29. I. Chrzanowski, "Ze wspomnien o Sienkiewiczu," quoted in *Kalendarz*, p. 211.

30. The American public learned of Zakopane from a sketch "A Polish Summer Resort" by Archibald Cary Coolidge, printed in *The Nation*, no. 1632, October 8, 1896, pp. 268–69. Coolidge included some information on Sienkiewicz as the most outstanding visitor of the resort. J. Curtin, who visited the writer nine times in Poland, was hospitably entertained by the novelist and was invited by him on a wonderful excursion. (*Memoirs*, pp. 658–61).

31. *Kalendarz*, pp. 234–35.

32. *The Outlook*, August 3, 1901, p. 823.

33. Letter to Adam Krechowiecki, November 22, 1902, in *Dziela*, vol. LV, p. 397. Cf. also A. Stawar, *op. cit.*, pp. 325–33.

34. Cf. *Dziela*, vol. XL, p. 105.

35. "Dispossessing the Poles," by Henryk Sienkiewicz and Emil Klaessig, "An Insult to Civilization," by Emil Klaessig, "The Polish Question" (editorial), *The Outlook*, vol. LXXXVII:10, March 7, 1908, pp. 541–44; 531–33. Cf. "Sienkiewicz's 'Political Duel'," by Mieczyslaw Giergielewicz, *The Polish Review*, vol. IX, 1964, no. 4, pp. 65–72.

36. Letter to J. Janczewska, after *Kalendarz*, p. 281.

Chapter Two

1 *Dziela*, vol. XLIV, pp. 58–59.

2. *Ibid.*, vol. XLVII, p. 93.

3. *Ibid.*, pp. 136–40.

4. *Ibid.*, vol. XLVIII, p. 192.

5. *Ibid.*, p. 55.

6. *Ibid.*, vol. XL, p. 234.

7. Cf. the preface of *Portrait of America; Letters of Henry Sienkiewicz*, edited and translated by Charles Morley (New York, 1959), pp. 14–15.

8. The valuable essay by Zdzislaw Najder on Sienkiewicz's American letters gives much information on the writer's trip. Some aspects of the California chapter of Sienkiewicz's expedition are discussed by A. P. and M. Coleman, *Wanderers Twain; Modjeska and Sienkiewicz: A View from California* (Cheshire, Conn., 1964).

9. Cf. A. P. and M. Coleman, *op. cit.*, pp. 42–43.

10. *Dziela*, vol. XLI, third letter, pp. 106–7.

11. *Ibid.*, p. 90.

12. *Ibid.*, letter of September 9, 1877 from San Francisco, vol. XLII, pp. 236–37.

13. *Ibid.*, vol. XLI, pp. 141–46.

14. *Ibid.*, vol. XLII, p. 50.

15. *Ibid.*, p. 51.

16. *Ibid.*, vol. XL, p. 185.

17. *Portrait of America, op. cit.*, p. 84.

18. *Ibid.*, pp. 175–76.

19. *Ibid.*, p. 176.

20. An amusing controversy refers to American women. According to Najder, ("O 'Listach z podrozy' do Ameryki . . . ," *op. cit.*, p. 39) Sienkiewicz "excessively idealized them and attributed to them subtlety and personal culture." Charles Morley contends that the novelist's harsher views underwent steady mellowing ". . . with the exception of those on American women." (*op. cit.*, Introduction, p. xvii.)

21. Letters from Paris in *Dziela*, vol. XLIV, p. 50.

22. *Ibid.*, p. 43.

23. *Ibid.*, pp. 49–50.

24. *Ibid.*, pp. 52–53.

25. Zdzislaw Najder devoted to African letters a separate essay "O 'Listach z Afryki' Henryka Sienkiewicza," *Pamietnik Literacki,* vol. XLVII:4, 1956, pp. 330–50.

26. Details of the African trip can be found in a letter to Edward Lubowski, *Dziela*, vol. LV, pp. 147–50; and to H. Siemiradzki, *ibid.*, vol. LVI, pp. 123–29.

27. Stefania Skwarczynska in her book *Teoria listu* (The Theory of the Letter, Lwow, 1937) makes a clear distinction between letters as means of communication and letters as a literary device.

Chapter Three

1. In the United States "Let Us Follow Him" was reprinted at least 30 times; "Hania," 10 times; and "Za Chlebem," 15 times (under different titles) .

2. "Hania," tr. by J. Curtin (Boston, 1897), p. 148. As to the adopted camouflage, see Jerzy Pietrkiewicz's "Inner Censorship in Polish Literature," *The Slavonic and East European Review* (London) , LXVI, 1958.

3. Later, however, Prus introduced a musical prodigy in his first novel *Placowka* (The Outpost) , published in 1885.

4. "Janko the Musician" in *Sielanka*, tr. by J. Curtin (Boston, 1898) , p. 262.

5. *Sielanka, op. cit.*, pp. 472–73.

6. The background of this story has been investigated by Jaroslaw Maciejowski, in his study, *Wielkopolskie opowiadania Henryka Sienkiewicza* (Poznan, 1957) .

7. Maciejowski, *op. cit.*, pp. 18–27. The critic pointed out that in the

initial plan the novelist introduced a peasant family from Mazovia and brought the tale to a happy end—Jasko would go to America and save his beloved girl from peril.

8. Quoted after Alina Nofer, *Henryk Sienkiewicz* (Warsaw, 1959), p. 136.

9. *Dziela,* vol. XLII, pp. 291–92.

10. "Across the Plains," *Sielanka, op. cit.,* pp. 365–66.

11. *Dziela,* vol. XLII, pp. 218–19.

12. In "Hania," tr by J. Curtin (Boston, 1897), pp. 389–91.

13. *Ibid.,* pp. 397–98.

14. *Book News,* vol. XXII, May 1904, pp. 972–73.

15. "Dwie laki" appeared as "A Hindoo Legend" in *Poet Lore,* vol. XV, 1904, pp. 48–51.

16. "The Wedding" was written in a similar vein.

17. Julius Mrosik recently called attention to a definition given by Goethe: "Denn was ist eine Novelle anders als eine sich ereignete Begebenheit," *Das polnische Bauerntum im Werke Eliza Orzeszkowas* (München, 1963), p. 24. Some technical aspects of the short story were discussed by Olga Scherer-Virski, *The Modern Polish Short Story* ('s-Gravenhage, 1955), pp. 3–6.

18. Olga Scherer-Virski values "Charcoal Sketches," "Yanko the Musician," and "Yamyol."

Chapter Four

1. The translation was written in the period of Slowacki's mysticism, when he identified his attitude toward Towianski with that of the Spanish hero.

2. A detailed confrontation of the *Trilogy* with Pasek is due to Julian Krzyzanowski's "Pasek i Sienkiewicz. Do zrodel *Trylogii,*" *Pamietnik Literacki,* vol. XLVII, 1965, pp. 301–32.

3. "O powiesci historycznej," *Dziela,* vol. XLV, pp. 106–10; 116–18.

4. Published in 1897. It was translated into English by J. Curtin (Boston, 1902). Prus's essay on Sienkiewicz was reprinted several times. Recently it appeared in Jodelka, *"Trylogia" H. Sienkiewicza,* pp. 166–96.

5. Samuel Sandler, *Wokol "Trylogii"* (Wroclaw, 1952), Jodelka, *op. cit.,* pp. 500–519. Cf. also his essay "Dalekie i bliskie Sienkiewiczowskiej *Trylogii,*" *Polonistyka,* no. 4, 1954, p. 3.

6. *Dziela,* vol. XLI, p. 190. An association with Ukraine also appears in vol. XLII, p. 8.

7. Parts of this essay were reprinted in Jodelka, *op. cit.,* pp. 372–402.

8. *Ibid.,* pp. 388–92.

9. Wladyslaw Tomkiewicz, "Historyczne wartosci *Ogniem i mieczem*" in T. Jodelka, *op. cit.,* pp. 409–16.

10. *With Fire and Sword,* tr. by J. Curtin (Boston, 1890), "Introduction," pp. xiv–xv. Sienkiewicz objected to Curtin's treatment of the Ukrainians and wrote him a letter expressing his displeasure:

As to the preface, a difference should have been stressed between the Ruthenians, and the Russians who at that time were called Muscovites and who constituted quite a separate state, while the Ruthenians were a part of the Polish Commonwealth.

The Ruthenians have considered themselves a separate nation. Forcibly converted after the fall of the Commonwealth to the Greek Church, they have preserved a separate language. They are persecuted now in Ukraine and generally in the Empire.

Naturally I communicate this information to you confidentially, as if it were published under my name, it would expose me as a Russian subject to persecution.

(In *Dziela,* vol. LV, p. 60, dated probably in 1892.) Curtin did not find it necessary to change his prefaces.

11. *Dziela,* vol. L, p. 122.

12. In this way the defeats at Zolte Wody and Pilawce were treated.

13. Some literary aspects of this motif were discussed by A. Stawar, *op. cit.,* pp. 116–17.

14. A. Asnyk, "Historyczna nowa szkola," *Dziela poetyckie,* edited by Z. Michalowski (Warsaw s. a.), vol. I, pp. 112–13.

15. On another occasion Czarniecki says that only the Commonwealth is great and in proportion to her all families are little. *The Deluge,* vol. XV. p. 5.

16. *Ibid.,* vol. XIV, p. 5.

17. *Ibid.,* vol. XV, p. 6.

18. *Ibid.,* vol. XIV, 1, p. 2.

19. *Ibid.,* vol. XIV, p. 6.

20. *Ibid.,* vol. XIV, p. 8.

21. *Ibid.,* vol. XV, p. 6.

22. *Ibid.,* vol. XV, p. 5.

23. *Pan Wolodyjowski,* in *Dziela,* vol. XVII, pp. 81–83 (a conversation of Pan Michael with Sobieski).

24. Cf. J. Maciejowski, *op. cit.*

25. Cf. Alojzy Sajkowski, *Krzysztof Opalinski, wojewoda poznanski* (Poznan, 1960), esp. pp. 221–28 and 239–43.

26. *Dziela,* vol. XVI, p. 9.

27. *Ibid.,* vol. XVI, p. 16.

28. The Walter Scott aspects of the *Trilogy* have been discussed by K. Wojciechowski, *Henryk Sienkiewicz* (Lwow-Warsaw, 1925).

29. *The Three Musketeers* was also followed by two other novels

divided by periods of twenty and thirty years, respectively.

30. A. Stawar raised various objections regarding the realism of the battle scenes; however, some of his criticisms could also be referred to Pasek, a participant and eyewitness of many battles.

31. *Dziela*, vol. XVI, p. 15.

32. *Without Dogma*, tr. by Iza Young (Boston, 1893), p. iv.

33. Zygmunt Szweykowski, *"Trylogia" Sienkiewicza* (Poznan, 1961), pp. 43–46.

34. Cf. S. Sandler, *op. cit.*, p. 516.

35. Cf. A. Stawar, *op. cit.*, pp. 134–39. The problem was also discussed by other critics.

36. Sakowicz became Governor of the Smolensk province and Treasurer of the Grand Duchy of Lithuania. *The Deluge*, IV, XIX.

37. Modjeska, *op. cit.*, pp. 296–303.

38. *Ibid.*, vol. XIX. Cf. also Stawar, *op. cit.*, pp. 137–39.

39. Thomas Hatton and Arthur H. Cleaver, *A Bibliography of the Periodical Works of Charles Dickens* (London, 1933), p. 3. Negative effects of serialization in Dickens's novels were pointed out by Emile Legouis in *A Short Story of English Literature* (Oxford, 1936), pp. 325–26.

40. Cf. Nora Atkinson, *Eugène Sue et le roman-feuilleton* (Paris, 1929), pp. 6–7; 12. The book of Alfred Nettement *Etudes critiques sur le feuilleton-roman* (Paris, 1847) was a voice of protest against this kind of novel writing.

41. This problem was discussed by David J. Welsh in his interesting essay "Serialization and Structure in the Novels of Henry Sienkiewicz," *The Polish Review*, vol. IX, nr. 3, 1964, pp. 51–62.

42. Cf. *Kalendarz*, pp. 111–12.

43. A description of Sienkiewicz's method of work is given by J. Curtin, *Memoirs*, *op. cit.*, pp. 647–48.

44. *Dziela*, vol. VII, p. 1.

45. *Ibid.*, p. 13.

46. *Ibid.*, p. 43.

47. *Ibid.*, p. 63.

48. *Ibid.*, p. 117.

49. *The Deluge, Dziela,* vol. XI, p. 6.

50. *Ibid.*, chapter 4, pp. 63–66; V, pp. 81–83.

51. *Ibid.*, vol. XIII, p. 10.

52. *Ibid.*, vol. XIII, p. 18.

53. Cf. a letter of Kmicic to Olenka, *ibid.*, vol. I, p. 6.

54 *Ibid.*, vol. XI, p. 9.

55. *Ibid.*, vol. I. p. 13.

56. *Ibid.*, vol. XVI.

57. *The Deluge,* tr. by Curtin, vol. II, p. 594. The translator uses *Kmita* for *Kmicic.*

58. Cf. Victor Erlich, *Russian Formalism; History—Doctrine* (s-Gravenhage, 1955), p. 276.

59. *Ibid.,* p. 212.

60. Cf. L. P. Grossman, "Dostoevski—khudozhnik," in *Tvorchestvo Dostoevskogo* (Moscow, 1959), p. 344.

61. *Dziela,* vol. VIII, chapter 17, pp. 255–57. It is the end of the second volume of the novel.

62. *Dziela,* vol. XV, chapters 12–13.

63. As to the esthetic meaning of the structure of chapters, cf. *Khudozhestvennaya proza, razmyshlenia i razbory,* by Viktor Shklovsky (Moscow, 1959), pp. 297–305; 460–66.

64. *Dziela,* vol. XIII, p. 10.

65. *Ibid.,* p. 5.

66. Cf. the eighteenth-century *Opis obyczajow za panowania Augusta III,* by Jedrzej Kitowicz, recently re-edited by Roman Pollak (Wroclaw, 1951), pp. 231–39, 341–42.

67. In T. Jodelka, *op. cit.,* p. 70.

68. J. Curtin, *Memoirs, op. cit.,* p. 531. The author speaks of his translation of *Quo Vadis?,* but this remark is applicable to other novels.

69. The American critics considered the *Trilogy* the greatest achievement of Sienkiewicz. One of the fine eulogies of this work was due to Annie Kimball Tuell in "Henryk Sienkiewicz," *The Catholic World,* CVII, April 1918, p. 21.

Chapter Five

1. Letter to J. Janczewska dated November 12, 1889, quoted after *Kalendarz,* p. 163.

2. Much attention was devoted to this tragedy in *Zygmunt Krasinski, Romantic Universalist; An International Tribute,* edited by Waclaw Lednicki (New York, 1964), esp. in the essays by W. Lednicki (pp. 155–81) and Czeslaw Milosz (pp. 212–22).

3. *Morituri* was published in 1874–75.

4. *Lalka* (The Doll) was at first serialized; its complete edition appeared in 1890.

5. *Without Dogma, op. cit.,* p. 70.

6. *Ibid.,* pp. 3–4.

7. *Ibid.,* p. 11.

8. *Ibid.,* p. 34.

9. *Ibid.,* p. 20.

10. *Ibid.,* p. 22.

Notes and References

11. "Henryk Sienkiewicz," by Piotr Chmielowski in his *Pisma krytycznoliterackie*, ed. by Henryk Markiewicz (Warsaw, 1961), pp. 527–30.

12. *Without Dogma, op. cit.*, p. 35.

13. *Ibid.*, pp. 343–44.

14. *Kalendarz*, p. 177. This opinion was confirmed by Curtin in his conversation on Sienkiewicz with Tolstoy. See Curtin, *Memoirs, op. cit.*, p. 787 (in 1900).

15. I. Gofshtetter, "Genrikh Sienkiewicz kak psikholog sovremennosti (Publichnaya lekciya)," *Russkaya Beseda*, vol. I, 1896, pp. 85–104.

16. Even Chmielowski spoke of this novel coolly and identified its protagonist with a crowd of money makers, heads of families indifferent to social needs. Chmielowski, *op. cit.*, p. 543.

17. *Ibid.*, p. 541.

18. Chmielowski attached the label "irony of life" to various developments of the novel. *Op. cit.*, pp. 546, 554, 555.

19. *Dziela*, vol. XXXIV, p. 163.

20. Plawicki plays a more prominent role in the first three chapters of the novel and later appears only occasionally.

21. Pisemskij's novel *V vodovorote* (In the Whirlpool) was written in 1871. Its heroine Elena Ziglinskaya was of Polish descent. Cf. Charles A. Moser, *Antinihilism in the Russian Novel of the 1860s* (The Hague, 1964), pp. 65–66.

22. *Whirlpools*, in *Dziela*, vol. XXXV, chapter 10, p. 185.

23. *The Polaniecki Family*, in *Dziela*, vol. XXXIV, chapter 27, p. 361.

24. *Whirlpools, op. cit.*, vol. XXXVI, p. 193.

25. *Ibid.*, vol. XXXV, pp. 31–34.

26. *Ibid.*, pp. 149–50.

Chapter Six

1. Alfons Bronarski, *Stosunek "Quo Vadis?" do literatur romanskich* (Poznan, 1926), with a rich bibliography on the subject, pp. 8–9. The French repercussions were examined by Maria Kosko, whose last book, *Un "best-seller" 1900—Quo Vadis?* (Paris, 1960), contains a comprehensive bibliographical review.

2. Bronarski, *op. cit.*, p. 7.

3. This information was due to Ferdynand Hoesick's *Powiesc mojego zycia* (Wroclaw-Krakow, 1959), vol. II, pp. 48–49. Cf. also Sienkiewicz's letter to Kazimierz Morawski, *Dziela*, vol. LV, p. 492.

4. This incident was reported by L. H. Morstin. Cf. A. Nofer, *op. cit.*, pp. 273–74

5. *Quo Vadis?*, tr. by J. Curtin (Boston, 1896), p. 316. Cf. the interesting observations on the urge to blur the boundary between art and

life in Victor Erlich, *The Double Image; Concepts of the Poet in Slavic Literatures* (Baltimore, 1964), pp. 56–58.

6. George McDermot, "Henryk Sienkiewicz," *The Catholic World*, vol. LXVI, February 1898, pp. 658–59.

7. *Quo Vadis?, op. cit.,* vol. II. p. 31.

8. *Ibid.,* vol. XIII, p. 115.

9. *Fabiola; or the Church of the Catacombs* (New York, 1858), pp. 12–13.

10. Konstanty Wojciechowski, *Henryk Sienkiewicz* (Lwow, 1925), pp. 92–93.

11. Alfons Bronarski, *"Quo Vadis?" H. Sienkiewicza i jego apologetyczne znaczenie* (Rome, 1960), p. 53 (with a French résumé, pp. 47–53).

12. The article of Konrad Gorski appeared in *Tygodnik Powszechny* (1946), nos. 19–60. Cf. A. Bronarski, *Quo Vadis? . . . , op. cit.,* p. 4.

13. *Ibid.,* pp. 4–5.

14. *Kalendarz,* pp. 201–2.

15. *Polskii istoricheskii roman i problema istorizma,* by I. K. Gorsky (Moscow, 1963), pp. 122–23.

16. "Henryk Sienkiewicz," by Edmund Gosse, *The Living Age,* XIV (CCXIII), May 22, 1897, pp. 526–27.

17. *Quo Vadis?,* tr. by J. Curtin, op. cit., I, p. 6.

18. *Ibid.,* XXXII, p. 260.

19. *Ibid.,* XXX, p. 250.

20. *Ibid.,* XXXVI, p. 293. These words appear at the end of the respective chapter.

21. *Ibid.,* LIX, p. 468.

22. *Ibid.,* XXXV, p. 284.

23. *Ibid.,* LXI, pp. 475–76.

24. *Dziela,* vol. XLVI, p. 69.

25. *Quo Vadis?, op. cit.,* vol. XLVIII, pp. 370–71.

26. J. Kaden Bandrowski, *Stefan Zeromski, prorok niepodleglosci* (Lwow, 1930). Quoted after *Przede wszystkim Sienkiewicz* by Zygmunt Falkowski (Warsaw, 1959), p. 87.

27. *Memoirs* by J. Curtin, *op. cit.,* pp. 530–31.

28. *Book News,* II, 1898, p. 367.

29. Quoted after Maria Kosko, *La fortune de "Quo vadis?" de Sienkiewicz en France* (Paris, 1935), p. 17.

30. *Good Reading* prepared by the Committee on College Reading and edited by J. Sherwood Weber includes *Quo Vadis?* in the section "Books About Rome," 15th printing, rev. ed. (New York, 1960), p. 37. The comment is not quite fair to Sienkiewicz.

31. *"Quo vadis?" H. Sienkiewicza . . . , op. cit.,* p. 17.

32. "Sienkiewicz' New Novel," by Nathan Haskell Dole, *The Book-man*, IV, 1986, p. 249.

Chapter Seven

1. Stefan Kuczynski, *Rzeczywistosc historyczna w "Krzyzakach" Hen-ryka Sienkiewicza* (Warsaw, 1963), pp. 190, 192. Some opinions on the author were discussed more recently by Juliusz Kijas, "Zrodla historyczne *Krzyzakow*," *Pamietnik Literacki*, vol LV, 1964, p. 3.
2. Cf. Kijas, *op. cit.*, pp. 86–87.
3. *Knights of the Cross*, tr. by J. Curtin (Boston, 1900), vol. I, p. 382.
4. *Ibid.*, vol. II, p. 262.
5. Antoni Golubiew, "Probuje odkryc Sienkiewicza," reprinted in T. Jodelka, *op. cit.*, pp. 428–34. A major literary event was an essay "Sprawa Sienkiewicza," *Tworczosc*, 1956, which raised contemporary aspects of the *Trilogy* (Jodelka, pp. 435–59).
6. A. Nofer, *op. cit.*, p. 312.

Chapter Eight

1. Curtin, *op. cit.*, p. 900.
2. Letter to W. Ulanowska in *Dziela*, vol. LVI, pp. 186–87.
3. Curtin attributed the shortening of *On the Field of Glory* to the Russo-Japanese War, which completely absorbed the writer. See *Memoirs*, p. 900.
4. Two fine essays were recently devoted to Sienkiewicz's novel for youth: *"W pustyni i w puszczy* Henryka Sienkiewicza," by K. Kuliczkow-ska, *Z literatury lat 1863–1918* (Wroclaw, 1957), pp. 287–352; and *"W pustyni i w puszczy* Henryka Sienkiewicza," by Andrzej Lange in *Pamietnik Literacki*, XLVII, 1956, pp. 351–88.

Chapter Nine

1. Many Polish critics contended on various occasions that the films based on *Quo Vadis?* did not do justice to the novelist and grossly vulgarized the content of his work. Cf. Zygmunt Nowakowski, "Kolosss-ssalne prostactwo" (A Colossal Vulgarity), in *Lajkonik na wygnaniu* (London, 1963), pp. 69–73.
2. Witold Gombrowicz, *Dziennik* (Diary, Paris, 1957), pp. 327–28, 334.
3. The fine essay by J. de Montherlant "Le roman défamé: *Quo Vadis?*" appeared in the French literary weekly *Les nouvelles littéraires* in 1961.

Selected Bibliography

I Primary Sources

Collective Edition in Polish

Dziela. Ed. by Julian Krzyzanowski. Warszawa: Panstwowy Instytut Wydawniczy, 1947–55. 60 vols.

English Translations (First Editions Only)

1. Novels

With Fire and Sword (Ogniem i mieczem). Tr. by Jeremiah Curtin. Boston: Little, Brown & Co., 1890.
————. Tr. by Samuel A. Binion. New York: Crowell, 1905.
The Deluge (Potop). Tr. by J. Curtin. Boston: Little, Brown & Co., 1893.
Pan Michael (Pan Wolodyjowski). Tr. by J. Curtin. Boston: Little, Brown & Co., 1893.
————. Tr. by S. A. Binion. New York: Crowell, 1898.
Without Dogma (Bez dogmatu). Tr. by Iza Young. Boston: Little, Brown & Co., 1893.
Children of the Soil (Rodzina Polanieckich). Tr. by J. Curtin. Boston: Little, Brown & Co., 1895.
The Irony of Life (Rodzina Polanieckich). Tr. by N. M. Babad. New York: Fenno, 1900.
Quo Vadis? A Narrative of the Time of Nero. Tr. by J. Curtin. Boston: Little, Brown & Co., 1896.
————. *A Tale of the Time of Nero.* Tr. by S. A. Binion and S. Malevsky. Philadelphia: H. Altemus, 1897.
————. *A Story of the Time of Nero.* Tr. by William E. Smith. New York: Ogilvie, 1898.
————. Tr. by C. J. Hogarth. New York: Nelson, 1914.
————. *A Tale of the Time of Nero.* Tr. by A. Heyman. Chicago: Donohue, s.a.
The Knights of the Cross (Krzyzacy). Part I. Tr. by S. C. de Soissons. New York: Fenno, 1897.
————. Tr. by J. Curtin. Boston: Little, Brown & Co., 1900. 2 vols.
————. Tr. by Samuel A. Binion. New York: Fenno, 1900. 3 vols.
————. (abridged). Tr. by B. Dahl. New York: Ogilvie, 1900.
————. (special translation). New York: Street & Smith, 1900. 2 vols.

The Teutonic Knights (Krzyzacy). Tr. by Alicja Tyszkiewicz. London: Thomas Nelson & Sons, 1943.

On the Field of Glory (Na polu chwaly). Tr. by J. Curtin. Boston: Little, Brown & Co., 1906.

The Field of Glory (Na polu chwaly). Tr. by Henry Britoff. New York: Ogilvie, 1906.

Whirlpools (Wiry). Tr. by Max A. Drezmal. Boston: Little, Brown & Co., 1910.

In Desert and Wilderness (W pustyni i puszczy). Tr. by M. A. Drezmal. Boston: Little, Brown & Co., 1912.

Through the Desert (W pustyni i puszczy). Tr. by Mary Webb Artois. New York: Benziger Bros., 1912.

2. Tales and Short Stories

"Paul" (Z pamietnika korepetytora). Tr. by W. R. Thompson. *The Catholic World,* IV (1884), 406–19.

Yanko the Musician and Other Stories. Tr. by J. Curtin. Boston: Little, Brown & Co., 1893. 5 stories.

Lillian Morris and Other Stories. Tr. by J. Curtin. Boston: Little, Brown & Co., 1894. 4 stories.

Hania. Tr. by J. Curtin. Boston: Little, Brown & Co., 1897, 11 stories.

Let Us Follow Him and Other Stories. Tr. by Vatslaf A. Hlasko and Thomas H. Bullick. New York: Fenno, 1897. 6 stories.

————. Tr. by Sigmund C. Slupski and I. Young. Philadelphia: H. Altemus, 1898. 3 stories.

Sielanka: A Forest Picture and Other Stories. Tr. by J. Curtin. Boston: Little, Brown & Co., 1898. 12 stories, 2 plays, and 3 essays.

For Daily Bread and Other Stories. Tr. by I. Young. Philadelphia: H. Altemus, 1898.

Tales. Tr. by S. C. de Soissons. London: Allen, 1901. 8 stories and 1 play.

Life and Death and Other Legends and Stories. Tr. by J. Curtin. Boston: Little, Brown & Co., 1904. 5 stories.

So Runs the World. Tr. by S. C. de Soissons. London: F. T. Neely, 1898. Stories and 2 plays.

Tales. Ed. by Monica Mary Gardner. New York: E. P. Dutton, 1931. Also, Everyman's Library, 871. 8 stories.

3. Plays

On a Single Card (Na jedna karte). Tr. by J. Curtin. (In *Sielanka* [see above], 175–254.)

Win or Lose (Na jedna karte). Tr. by S. C. de Soissons. (In *So Runs the World* [see above], 153–290.)

Selected Bibliography

Whose Fault? (Czyja wina?). Tr. by J. Curtin. (In *Sielanka* [see above], 139–56.)

——. Tr. by S. C. de Soissons. (In *So Runs the World* [see above], 89–123; also in Tales [see above], 217–42.)

I Must Take a Rest (Musze wypoczac). Tr. anon. *Current Literature*, XLI (July, 1906). 114–16.

4. Letters from America

"American Sketches." Tr. anon. *The Living Age*, CCCXIII (June 24, 1922), 757–63 (subtitles: "New York Hotels," "Broadway," "Chicago," "Customs and Manners," "American Women"; and CCCXIV (July 1, 1922), 23–29 (subtitle: "Forest Life in America").

"Letters from America." Tr. by Casimir Gonski. *Poland*, VII (Jan., 1926), 28 (Feb.), 92–94, 114–18 (Mar.), 156–59, 180–89 (Apr.,) 214–15, 227 (May), 280–81, 322–24.

"Out of the Desert Came the Santa Ana and Anaheim Landing: A Fisherman's Paradise." Tr. by Eda and Ruth Zakheim. *Westways*, XXXVIII (Feb. and March, 1946), 18–19; 22–23.

"That Was the West: My First Visit to Virginia City." Tr. by Ronald Strom. *Territorial Entreprise and Virginia City News* (Virginia City, Nev.), CII, 8 (Feb. 25, 1955), 5 (Mar. 4), 5 (Mar. 11), 11, 14.

"The Chinese in California." Tr. by Charles Morley. *California Historical Society Quarterly*, XXXIV (Dec. 1955), 301–16.

Portrait of America; Letters. Tr. by Charles Morley. New York: Columbia University Press, 1959.

II Selective Secondary Sources

Note: This bibliography contains only a fraction of the critical material devoted to Sienkiewicz. The serious student should consult other bibliographies. The most comprehensive one has been included in volume LX of *Dziela* (see above), which lists over 3,800 items.

1. English

BIRKENMAJER, JOZEF. "Henryk Sienkiewicz." *Thought; Quarterly of the Sciences and Letters*. V. XIV, 55 (Dec., 1939), 579–93. Brief biographical sketch stressing the writer's psychological insight and defending Zagloba as one of the most renowned humorous characters.

COLEMAN, ARTHUR PRUDDEN and MARION MOORE. *Wanderers Twain*. Cheshire, Conn.: Cherry Hill Books, 1964. A sentimental sketch about the stay of Sienkiewicz and the famous actress H. Modjeska in California.

COLLECTIVE. "Dispossessing the Poles." *The Outlook*, LXXXVIII (Mar. 7, 1908), 531-33, 542-44. Sienkiewicz's protest against Prussian land policy with reply by German opponent, and editorial supporting the view of the Polish novelist.

CURTIN, JEREMIAH. *Memoirs*. Madison: State Historical Society of Wisconsin, 1940. Contains reminiscences of ten meetings with Sienkiewicz and reports of their conversations; a valuable source for biographers of the novelist.

DOLE, NATHAN HASKELL. "Sienkiewicz's New Novel." *The Bookman*, IX, 3 (Nov., 1896), 248-50. One of the earliest reviews of *Quo Vadis?* in America defining the novel as the most fascinating and absorbing reading.

FINDLATER, JANE. "Great War Novels." *Living Age*, CCXXX (Aug. 24, 1901), 488-96. Qualifies the *Trilogy* as an outstanding example of the modern war novel comparable to the works of Zola and Tolstoy, but preserving the spirit of the ancient epic.

GARDNER, MONICA. *The Patriot Novelist of Poland Henryk Sienkiewicz*. London: J. M. Dent, 1926. An emotional appraisal of the writer and his patriotic message, based mainly on the *Trilogy*.

GIERGIELEWICZ, MIECZYSLAW. "Henryk Sienkiewicz's American Resonance." *Antemurale*, X, 1966 (Rome), 256-354. A comprehensive review of Sienkiewicz's repercussions in American criticism, with a bibliography.

GOSSE, EDMUND. "Henryk Sienkiewicz." *Living Age* (reprint from *The Contemporary Review*), 6th Ser., XIV (CCXIII) (May 22, 1897), 517-27. A sober estimate of Sienkiewicz's works: laudatory about the *Trilogy*, severe toward *Quo Vadis?* (which the critic did not read), critical of the translator.

KOWALCZYK, STANLEY ANTHONY. "Some Historical and Literary Aspects of Henryk Sienkiewicz's *With Fire and Sword*". Unpubl. diss. (Univ. of Pa., 1952). Confronts the novel with the history of the Polish-Ukrainian conflict.

LECHON, JAN. "The Elderly Gentleman with the Rose." *Bulletin of the Polish Institute of Arts and Sciences*, IV (1945-46), 79-82. Develops the idea that the novelist, unlike other writers, escaped from the burning problems of his generation into the past, thereby earning applause.

LEDNICKI, WACLAW. *Bits of Table Talk on Pushkin, Mickiewicz, Goethe, Turgenev and Sienkiewicz*. The Hague: Martinus Nijhoff, 1956. A fine commentary on the novelist's major works.

————. *Henryk Sienkiewicz: A Retrospective Synthesis*. s'Gravenhage: Mouton, 1960. A carefully measured attempt to mark out the stature of the writer in the history of literature, brightened

Selected Bibliography

by the reminiscences of the critic's meeting with Sienkiewicz.

McDermot, C. P. S. "Henryk Sienkiewicz." *The Catholic World*, LXVI (Feb., 1898), 652–61; LXVII (May, 1898), 180–91. Analysis of *Without Dogma* and *Quo Vadis* with an ingenious comparison of the two novels; confronts them with Shakespeare, Byron, and Goethe. As to the *Trilogy*, Zagloba is compared with Falstaff; some connections with *Don Quixote* are stressed.

Modjeska (Modrzejewska), Helena. *Memories and Impressions; an Autobiography*. New York: Macmillan, 1910. Some reminiscences of the actress refer to her acquaintance with Sienkiewicz in Warsaw, their idea of a settlement in California, and its subsequent failure.

Phelps, William Lyon. *Essays on Modern Novelists*. New York: Macmillan, 1910. Includes a brief but skilfully worded outline of Sienkiewicz's literary contribution to world literature.

Scherer-Virski, Olga. *The Modern Polish Short Story*. s'Gravenhage: Mouton, 1955. The passages on Sienkiewicz discuss the technical aspects of his selected short stories.

De Soissons, S. C. "Henryk Sienkiewicz and His Writings." *North American Review*, CLXXV (Aug., 1908). A brief but interesting review of Sienkiewicz's works on a comparative background; considers *The Teutonic Knights* a true heroic poem.

Tuell, Annie Kimball. "Henryk Sienkiewicz." *The Catholic World*, CVII (April, 1918), 17–31. This fine essay concentrates on the novelist's works with a Polish background and tries to define their moral mood and general message; contains refreshing observations and still worthy of attention.

Welsh, David J. "Serialization and Structure in the Novels of Henryk Sienkiewicz." *The Polish Review*, IX (1964) No. 3, 51–62. An attempt to explain some structural devices of the novelist's major works by the author's habit of publishing them in short instalments.

2. Polish

Baculewski, Jan. *Henryk Sienkiewicz*. Warszawa: Wiedza Powszechna, 1958. Popular biography and brief review of Sienkiewicz's literary heritage; reflects opinions prevailing in contemporary Poland.

Bronarski, Alfons. *'Quo Vadis?' Henryka Sienkiewicza i jego apologetyczne znaczenie*. Rzym, 1960. Study of the controversy among Catholic writers on the moral values in Sienkiewicz's most renowned novel; an attempt to represent it as a Christian work. (Résumé in French.)

——. *Stosunek 'Quo Vadis?' do literatur romanskich*. Poznan:

naklad Poznanskiego Tow. Przyjaciol Nauk, 1926. Describes the relationship between *Quo Vadis?* and the romance literatures, mainly French and Italian.

BUJNICKI, TADEUSZ. "Mala trylogia Henryka Sienkiewicza." *Prace Historycznoliterackie*, 4 (Krakow: Uniw. Jagiellonski, 1961), 63–104. (*Résumé* in English, 104–105.) Essay on "The Old Servant," "Hania," and "Selim Mirza."

————. "Szkice weglem Henryka Sienkiewicza." *Pamietnik Literacki*, LIV:1 (1963), 33–62. A reappraisal of "Charcoal Sketches" as a turning point in the development of Sienkiewicz's craftsmanship.

BUKOWIECKI, JACEK. "Pierwszy artykul polityczny Henryka Sienkiewicza." *Wiadomosci* (London 1965), 4:982. A Polish translation of the novelist's article on Poland hitherto unknown.

CHMIELOWSKI, PIOTR. "Henryk Sienkiewicz w oswietleniu krytycznym," in *Pisma krytyczno-literackie*, Warszawa: Państwowy Instytut Wydawn., 1961. An analytical appraisal written by one of Sienkiewicz's contemporaries, a prominent literary historian.

CZACHOWSKI, KAZIMIERZ. *Henryk Sienkiewicz: obraz tworczosci*. Warszawa, 1931. An anthology of essays on Sienkiewicz, with a rich bibliography.

FALKOWSKI, ZYGMUNT. *Przede wszystkim Sienkiewicz*. Warszawa: Pax, 1959. An unbalanced, but impressive review of the controversies provoked by the writer; asserts that the novelist raised his fiction to the level of a national epic.

GORKA, OLGIERD. *'Ogniem i mieczem' a rzeczywistosc historyczna*. Warszawa, 1934. Pointing out to discrepancies between the novel and history, this book inaugurated long and bitter strife.

JAKUBOWSKI, JAN Z. et al. *Dziedzictwo literackie powstania styczniowego*. Warszawa, 1964. Includes two essays by J. Krzyzanowski tracing the echoes of January uprising (1863–64) in Sienkiewicz's works.

JODELKA, TOMASZ, Ed. *"Trylogia" Henryka Sienkiewicza: studia, szkice, polemiki*. Warszawa: Panstwowy Instytut Wydawn., 1962. A carefully selected anthology of the repercussions of the *Trilogy* in Polish literary life.

KRZYZANOWSKI, JULIAN. *Henryka Sienkiewicza zywot i sprawy*. Warszawa, Panstw. Inst. Wyd., 1966. A lively biography of the writer, clarifying various obscure episodes of his life, with many illustrations.

KUCZYNSKI, STEFAN. *Rzeczywistosc historyczna w 'Krzyzakach' Henryka Sienkiewicza*. Warszawa: Panstwowy Inst. Wyd., 1963. A confrontation of *The Teutonic Knights* with contemporary historical knowledge of the epoch concerned.

KULCZYCKA-SALONI, JANINA. "Henryk Sienkiewicz: krytyk i teoretyk literatury." *Pamietnik Literacki*, XLVII:4 (1956), 389–444. A review

Selected Bibliography

of the writer's opinions on literature and his literary criticism.

KULICZKOWSKA, K. "*W pustyni i w puszczy* Henryka Sienkiewicza." In *Z literatury lat 1863–1918*. Wroclaw, Zakl. Narodowy im. Ossolinskich, 1963. Analyzes the author's novel for youth.

MACIEJOWSKI, JAROSLAW. "*Wielkopolskie" opowiadania Henryka Sienkiewicza*. Poznan: Poznanskie Wyd. Naukowe, 1957. Clarifies the political and social background of the short stories dealing with the Prussian partition of Poland.

NAJDER, ZDZISLAW. "O *Listach z podrozy do Ameryki* Henryka Sienkiewicza." *Pamietnik Literacki*, XLVI:1 (1955), 54–122. On historical, social, and esthetic aspects of *Letters from America*.

NOFER, ALINA. *Henryk Sienkiewicz*. Warszawa:Wiedza Powszechna, 1959. Popular survey of novelist's life and works exalting *The Teutonic Knights* and critical of *Quo Vadis?*

PAPEE, STEFAN. *Henryk Sienkiewicz jako humorysta*. Lwow: Panstwowe Wydawn. Ksiazek Szkolnych, 1939 (Wyd. 2). A thorough study of humor in the works of Sienkiewicz.

SANDLER, SAMUEL. *Wokol 'Trylogii.'* Wroclaw: Zaklad Narodowy Im. Ossolinskich, 1952. A Marxist critic dispels the antagonism toward Sienkiewicz and encourages a positive attitude toward the *Trilogy*.

STAWAR, ANDRZEJ. *Pisarstwo Henryka Sienkiewicza*. Warszawa: Panstwowy Instytut Wydawn., 1960. An ambitious attempt by a Marxist critic, who was not a literary historian, to reassess Sienkiewicz's whole literary heritage. Though lacking methodical cohesion, it adds some refreshing and ingenious remarks.

SZWEYKOWSKI, ZYGMUNT. '*Trylogia*' *Sienkiewicza; szkice*. Poznan: Wydawn. Poznanskie, 1961. Attributes to the *Trilogy* a fairy-tale character and points out various technical devices supporting this conjecture.

TARNOWSKI, STANISLAW. *Henryk Sienkiewicz; studia do historii literatury polskiej*, v. 5, w. XIX. Krakow: Spolka Wydawn. Polska, 1897. Written by a prominent historian of literature who was one of the leaders of the conservatives, the book reflects the enthusiastic reception of the novelist among his contemporaries.

WOJCIECHOWSKI, KONSTANTY. *Henryk Sienkiewicz*. Lwow: Ksiaznica-Atlas, 1925. Written in a popular vein, giving many insights into author's technique and structural devices.

ZAWODZINSKI, KAROL WIKTOR. "Czy i dlaczego *Rodzina Polanieckich* jest martwa pozycja w dorobku Sienkiewicza?" In *Opowieści o powiesci*, Krakow: Wydawnictwo Literackie, 1963. A severe verdict on one of Sienkiewicz's contemporary novels, which the critic considers outdated.

————. "Wsrod nieznanych powiesci Sienkiewicza. (*Na polu chwaly*)."

Pamietnik Literacki, XL (1952), 129–44. In defense of *On the Field of Glory*, a historical novel relatively little known.

ZIOMEK, JERZY. "Bibliografia rocznicy Sienkiewiczowskiej [1946]." *Pamietnik Literacki*, XXXVII (1947), 293–300. A list of publications on the occasion of Sienkiewicz's centennial.

Other Sienkiewicziana printed in *Pamietnik Literacki* may be located in *Bibliografia 'Pamietnika Literackiego'*, 1946–62, by Jan Gawalkiewicz. Wroclaw: Zaklad Narodowy im. Ossolinskich, 1964; see also *Notes* of this book.

3. Other Languages

French:

BRONARSKI, ALPHONSE. "Les triomphes de *Quo vadis?* à l'étranger." *Les Amis de la Pologne*, 12 (1924). The story of the international success achieved by Sienkiewicz.

BORDEAUX, HENRI. "Les livres et les moeurs, M. Henryk Sienkiewicz: *Quo vadis?*" *La revue hebdomadaire* (Aug. 18, 1900), 419–32. An analytical study of the novel.

JEANROY, FÉLIX V. "Henri Sienkiewicz." In *Ecrivains célèbres de l'Europe contemporaine* (Paris, 1903). Defines *Quo Vadis?* as a novel of adventure and questions its originality.

KOSKO, MARIA. *La fortune de 'Quo vadis? de Sienkiewicz en France*. Paris: L. Rodstein, 1935. A fascinating study of the hostility of the French critics toward a successful foreign writer, with bibliographical data.

―――. *Un "best-seller" 1900: "Quo Vadis?,"* Paris: J. Corti, 1960. A revised version of the preceding book, with an excellent bibliography.

MARGUERITE, DENIS. "Sienkiewicz." *L'instantané, supplément illustré de la Revue hebdomadaire*, 12 (1917), 522–36.

MONTHERLANT, HENRI DE. "Le roman défamé; *Quo vadis?*," *Les Nouvelles Littéraires* (1961). The famous French writer speaks in defense of Sienkiewicz and stresses the literary value of *Quo vadis?*

PONTCRAY, J. DU. "Sienkiewicz et la littérature polonaise." *La revue slave*, I (1906), 150–70, 344–61.

Italian:

BERSANO BEGEY, MARINA. "La fortuna di Enrico Sienkiewicz." *Nel centenario di Sienkiewicz 1846–1946*, (Rome, 1946). An authoritative study of the novelist's reception in Italy.

Russian:

FEMELIDI, A. M. *Genrikh Senkevich, ego literaturnaia epokha, zhizn'*

Selected Bibliography

trudy i mysli. Peterburg: Vol'f, 1912. Probably the most ambitious and comprehensive prerevolutionary book in Russian on the Polish novelist.

GOFSHTETTER, I. "Genrikh Senkevich kak psikholog sovremennosti," (Publichnaia lekciia). *Russkaia beseda*, I, 1896, 85–104. Values highly *Without Dogma* and severely criticizes *The Polaniecki Family*.

GORSKY, IVAN KONSTANTINOVICH. *Polskii roman i problema istorizma*. Moskva, Izd-vo Akad. Nauk SSSR, 1963. Includes a review of Sienkiewicz's novels against comparative background; a spirited apology of *Quo vadis?* as a work with a revolutionary message.

OBOLEVICH, VIACHESLAV BORISOVICH. *Istoria polskoi literatury*. Leningrad, 1960. Out of twelve pages on Sienkiewicz, six are devoted to *The Teutonic Knights*, which Obolevich considers Sienkiewicz's masterpiece.

Index

Index

Index